Halakhic Man, Authentic Jew

Halakhic Man, Authentic Jew

Modern Expressions of Orthodox Thought from Rabbi Joseph B. Soloveitchik and Rabbi Eliezer Berkovits

Ira Bedzow

Urim Publications
Jerusalem • New York

Halakhic Man, Authentic Jew:
Modern Expressions of Orthodox Thought from Rabbi Joseph B. Soloveitchik and Rabbi Eliezer Berkovits
By Ira Bedzow

Printed in Israel. First Edition.
ISBN 13: 978-965-524-029-0
Urim Publications
P.O. Box 52287, Jerusalem 91521 Israel

Lambda Publishers Inc.
527 Empire Blvd., Brooklyn, New York 11225 U.S.A.
Tel: 718-972-5449 Fax: 718-972-6307, mh@ejudaica.com

www.UrimPublications.com

אודה ה׳ בכל לבי　אספרה כל נפלאותיך
דרך ה׳ מודיעני　ומלמד ארחותיך

אבי איש בתוך גיבורים　צדק ומשפט בידו
חתני הוא הולך תמים　ודובר אמת בלבבו

אמי לביאה מגנה　בחיבה רבתה גוריה
חתנתי גפן שתולה　ממים רבים פוריה

יד חזקה מחזקני　נקרב בזרוע נטויה
ובגלל אשתי כנפשי　ביתי ישיר הללויה

CONTENTS

INTRODUCTION

BEING A MODERN ORTHODOX JEW is not about trying to maintain the unstable equilibrium of preserving the psychology of traditional Jewish society in the pre-modern era while at the same time immersing oneself in the culture and identity of modern society. To pretend that the way a Jew lives and thinks about life today is the same as the way Jews lived and thought about life in a seventeenth-century European *shtetl* is not only to avoid the cognitive dissonance such an idea creates but to ignore self-reflection vis-à-vis one's environment. Neither could Modern Orthodoxy be a fusion of contemporary and orthodox thought, for modernism and postmodernism, which call for a reexamination of every aspect of existence and assert a distrust of convention, directly contradict orthodoxy, which hails traditional conceptions as dogma and rejects any potential replacements as heresy.

Modern Orthodoxy, as the order of any similar compound word implies, is primarily orthodox thought; it accepts the general traditional concepts of Judaism and promotes traditional Jewish norms of living. The difference between a standard orthodoxy and its modern counterpart is not in accepting or rejecting traditional concepts, but rather in the manner in which they interpret those concepts and the framework in which they place them. Modern Orthodox thought attempts to explain Judaism through the use of modern terminology and philosophical schools of thought with the hope that the self-reflecting Jew living according to traditional Jewish concepts will be able to understand his way of life vis-à-vis the modern world in which he lives, epitomizing the expression that the Torah speaks in the language of man. Because all translations from one contextual background to another necessarily entail alteration and revision for concepts to fit in the new framework, however, certain Modern Orthodox interpretations of traditional concepts may diverge from their original understanding.

Two Modern Orthodox thinkers of the previous generation shaped, and continue to shape, the contemporary Jew's perception of what it is to be Orthodox in the modern world. Both received a traditional education which was complemented with a doctorate in philosophy, immigrated to America to teach at a Modern Orthodox seminary, and currently have institutions dedicated to their thought. Rabbi Joseph Soloveitchik, the better known of the two thinkers, served as the director of the Rabbi Isaac Elchanan Theological Seminary at Yeshiva University, where he ordained close to two thousand Modern Orthodox rabbis who have spread their teacher's ideas to the communities they lead. Rabbi Eliezer Berkovits, who taught at the Hebrew Theological College in Chicago, was a prolific and controversial writer, and has been esteemed as possibly the most significant Jewish moral theorist of the last generation.[1]

This study cautiously attempts to examine the thought of both Rabbi Soloveitchik[2] and Rabbi Berkovits in order to determine how their philosophical language translated certain themes in the Jewish tradition into the philosophical parlance with which they expressed them and the implications of their translations. This study does not seek to "challenge a lion after his death" but not for fear that he may have had answers to refute any contention.[3] Rather, like a troubled student who refuses to say that he understands when he does not,[4] the objective is to review these great rabbis' works with the hope that it is seen with the perspective that a small student's questions may sharpens a teacher's mind until he extracts from him wondrous wisdom.[5] If such a perspective is not taken, then I am

---

[1] "Eliezer Berkovits and the Revival of Jewish Moral Thought," 24.

[2] Although Rabbi Soloveitchik's writings vary in style and theme, I assume, like Marvin Fox, that there is a general unity to his works, and one is able to ascertain common themes throughout his writings.

[3] BT *Gittin* 83a.

[4] *Hilkhot Talmud Torah* 4:4.

[5] *Hilkhot Talmud Torah* 5:13.

left with the reply, "Explain to me your honorable Torah, for my knowledge is limited and I want to stand upon the truth of the matter."[6] Looking at both their image of the model Jew and their understanding of Halakha, this survey will analyze their respective views on their own terms and in how they relate to the traditional sources.

[6] *Teshuvat Maharlbah* (Rabbi Levi ben Habib), Siman 126.

RABBI SOLOVEITCHIK AND THE HALAKHIC MAN

RABBI SOLOVEITCHIK[1] discusses his view of man in many of his writings and lectures, yet the most thorough analysis of what he sees as man's dialectical existence and its unification within the confines of Halakha takes place in "The Lonely Man of Faith" and *Halakhic Man*. Therefore, while other works may be referenced to give further elucidation, the main presentation of his idea will be through the backdrop of these two texts.

In his essay, "The Lonely Man of Faith," Rabbi Soloveitchik uses the dual account of creation in Genesis as a biblical testament to his bifurcated conception of man. Although each typology exists within every person, "the two accounts deal with two Adams, two men, two fathers of mankind, two types, two representatives of humanity, and it is no wonder that they are not identical."[2] While each man-type creates a community in which he can self-actualize, this divided existence does not allow him to realize his true being, thus causing existential loneliness. Contemporary man, due to the

---

[1] There is a disagreement regarding whether Rabbi Soloveitchik believed that the halakhic man was an ideal to be emulated or a description of a certain character type found in the world of the Lithuanian yeshivas. Those who argue that it is a description support their claim by stating that Rabbi Soloveitchik did not attempt to live up to the standards that he attributes to the halakhic man. However, because his writings focus repetitively on the character-type of the halakhic man, albeit in variegated forms, it would seem that the halakhic man is the central ideal figure of his religious philosophy. The disparity between the ideal halakhic man and other men is the same as that of the ideal theoretical Halakha and its practical counterpart. The fact that they do not correspond tells of an imperfection in reality and not a mistake in the ideal conception.

[2] "Lonely Man of Faith," 10.

values of modern society, is in a more precarious existential position than a person in any other society in history and, thus, he is the loneliest of all men. The only way for man to realize his true value and to understand his position within creation is to conflate the two typologies under the unifying ethico-moral norm of Halakha.

Rabbi Soloveitchik names these two typologies differently, depending on the broader framework of the particular discussion. Hence, for the purposes of understanding his conception of bifurcated man and to maintain consistency, we will call these two typologies epistemological man and ontological man. Epistemological man was created in the first account in Genesis.

> So Elohim[3] created man in His own image, in the image of Elohim created He him, male and female created He them. And Elohim blessed them and Elohim said unto them, be fruitful and multiply, and fill the earth and subdue it, and have dominion over fish of the sea, over the fowl of the heaven, and over the beasts, and all over the earth.[4]

Created in the image of Elohim, which Rabbi Soloveitchik defines as man's inner charismatic endowment as a creative being,[5] where creative means creating and not imaginative, epistemological man was blessed to procreate and to dominate the world. Domination, however, is not in essence a physical act of subordinating the world to man; rather, it is an intellectual comprehension of the world by man. Using the mathematical scientist as his model,[6] he describes the focus of epistemological man as follows, "Adam the first is interested in just a single aspect of reality and asks one question only – 'How does the cosmos function?' He is not fascinated by the

---

[3] My reason for using the terms "Elohim" and "Hashem" instead of "God" and "Lord" is to differentiate between each aspect of God and to show how each aspect influences man differently.

[4] Genesis 1:27–28.

[5] "Lonely Man of Faith," 12.

[6] "Lonely Man of Faith," 18.

question, 'Why does the cosmos function at all?' nor is he interested in the question, 'What is its essence?'"[7] The motive of the scientist who inquires of the function of the cosmos differs from that of the engineer. An engineer applies abstract knowledge in order to construct something in the physical world. He has a practical, material motivation. On the other hand, a scientist – and especially a theoretical scientist – does not want to apply his theories to a practical, material effect. His creativity and domination lie in the comprehension of his object of study, not in its practical manipulation. As a true imitator of Elohim, he understands that in the context of creation, the physical act is only a consequence of a previous thought.[8]

Epistemological man's creation is therefore the scientific or aesthetic laws which he can impose upon the natural world; the technological advances that he is able to invent thereafter are only manifestations of his creation. His understanding of the cosmos is based upon the accuracy of his model; the better the model can imitate the natural world, the better he understands it. Thus, as Rabbi Soloveitchik writes, "To be precise, his question is related not to the genuine functioning of the cosmos in itself but to the possibility of reproducing the dynamics of the cosmos by employing quantified-mathematized media which man evolves through postulation and creative thinking."[9] One may wonder how it is possible that epistemological man does not understand the genuine functioning of the cosmos since, as Rabbi Soloveitchik argues in his discussion of the necessity of confession, one can not truly understand the essence of his object of study without attempting to convert the observation into a communicable form, such as a mathematical formula or even simple language.

---

7 "Lonely Man of Faith," 13.

8 This concept is found in the liturgical poem "*Lekha Dodi*" by Rabbi Shlomo ha-Levi Alkabetz, which is sung during the Friday evening service that welcomes the Sabbath.

9 "Lonely Man of Faith," 13.

> Feelings, emotions, thoughts and ideas become clear, and are grasped only after they are expressed in sentences bearing a logical and grammatical structure. As long as one's thoughts remain repressed, as long as one has not brought them out into the open, no matter how sublime or exalted they may be, they are not truly yours; they are foreign and elusive.[10]

Describing a phenomenon is the only true way that one can understand it. Merely experiencing it without putting it into words is to let it go by uncomprehended. The key to understanding the difference between the scientist's artificial understanding via a mathematical formula and the genuine understanding produced by the penitent's confessional formula is the communicator's position in relation to that which he is communicating. The penitent expresses an idea of which he is an integral part, while epistemological man describes an object of study to which he sees himself as an outside observer. To communicate a personal confession is an expression of what one sees as real.[11] To communicate a description of the world via a mathematical formula or a work of art can only be recognized as analogy and metaphor rather than a true expression of the essence of reality.

Because of his limited ability and utilitarian disposition, epistemological man is social by nature. However, his sociability remains only on the level of functional practicality and does not threaten his goal of domination by impinging on his self-awareness as an independent being. It is a forced sociability that stems from the necessity of joint action in light of man's individual helplessness against a hostile world. As the story of Adam's creation shows, Adam was created in a society of individuals. "They, Adam and Eve, act together, work together, pursue common objectives

---

[10] *On Repentance*, 92.

[11] We will see later in the chapter how even the communication of a personal experience may be perverted, through the use of language, into a metaphor or gross generalization.

together; yet they do not exist together. Ontologically, they do not belong to each other; each is provided with an 'I' awareness and knows nothing of a 'We' awareness."[12] Epistemological man's community is a material, cultural one which defines its success in how it can rise above the natural world to create the artificial one in which it lives.

The ideal for which epistemological man strives, which affirms his individuality in the midst of a community, is dignity (*kavod*). Since a social, functional being will only hold as an ideal that to which he can relate, dignity must be a social, functional value that can be measured by what one has accomplished. In Rabbi Soloveitchik's words, "Dignity is a social and behavioral category, expressing not an intrinsic existential quality but a technique of living, a way of impressing society, the knowhow of commanding respect and attention of the other fellow, a capacity to make one's presence felt."[13] Dignity is superficial not only because it measures a person's accomplishments rather than the person himself, but also because it objectifies the person since he shows himself to others in the same way that he sees the world. Only external action can be measured and copied. Internal motivation remains outside the realm of analysis. Thus, dignity is the great paradox of epistemological man. As an individual in society, he acquires dignity through his actions toward others, who bestow dignity upon him. It affirms his individuality and his sociability at the same time.

Although Rabbi Soloveitchik associates dignity with a sense of responsibility, he is not referring to a moral responsibility, as some have maintained,[14] unless the sense of morality is functional and utilitarian rather than of higher ethical principles and values. The idea Rabbi Soloveitchik suggests – that a man who has less mastery over his environment is less responsible and therefore less dignified – can imply that one who is able is morally obligated to take care of

---

[12] "Lonely Man of Faith," 33.
[13] "Lonely Man of Faith," 25–26.
[14] "Rabbi Joseph Dov Soloveitchik and the Role of the Ethical," 16.

others who cannot care for themselves. Yet one must ask: how is the person of today, who can travel from Boston to New York by air, more morally responsible than someone of a previous century, who had to travel by car or by horse and buggy? How can the dignity and responsibility of one who can fight disease be compared to one who cannot when the two people do not live in the same generation? For whom is modern man responsible? He cannot be responsible for people of previous generations, for they cannot bestow upon him the dignity he desires simply because they are no longer alive.

Responsibility in this context can only mean freedom to act as one desires. It is a responsibility to oneself to fulfill what one has set out to do. As Rabbi Soloveitchik writes, "Dignity of man expressing itself in the awareness of being responsible and of being capable of discharging his responsibility cannot be realized as long as he has not gained mastery over his environment. For life in bondage to insensate elemental forces is a non-responsible and hence undignified affair."[15] Just as a president of the company has both more responsibility and more freedom to make his firm more successful than his secretary does and, as such, holds a more dignified position in the company hierarchy, modern man is more dignified than men of previous ages when viewed through the Vulgar Marxist belief of economic determinism.

Unlike epistemological man, ontological man does not use the knowledge of the world that he acquired through objective analysis as a means for creative domination. He is fascinated by the unknown, and the knowledge of the world that he seeks stems from his subjective experience. As the description of his creation portrays, he is truly a part of the world that he questions.

> And Hashem Elohim formed the man of the dust of the ground and breathed into his nostrils the breath of life and man became a living soul. And Hashem Elohim planted a garden eastward in Eden.... And Hashem Elohim took the

[15] "Lonely Man of Faith," 17.

> man and placed him in the Garden to serve it and to keep it.[16]

He is the phenomenologist par excellence. He knows the world because he was formed by it, and therefore, his understanding of the world comes from his sensory perception. He can not take himself outside of his analysis in order to create sterile objectivity. Instead, he sees the world as a real subject. As Rabbi Soloveitchik describes it,

> He encounters the universe in all its colorfulness, splendor, and grandeur, and studies it with the naïveté, awe and admiration of the child who seeks the unusual and wonderful in every ordinary thing and event. He looks for the image of God not in the mathematical formula or the natural relational law but in every beam of light, in every bud and blossom, in the morning breeze and the stillness of a starlit evening.[17]

For Rabbi Soloveitchik, the phrase "the image of God" in the above excerpt does not refer to the world's inner charismatic endowment as a creative being. Rather, it is the divine imprint of the Creator within His creation. As all creative artists indelibly leave their mark upon their work, the image of God, who is the Cause of all causes, is the reflection of God's creative attribute.[18]

God endowed ontological man with the breath of life. Therefore, only ontological man can sense the divinity within creation by virtue of its presence within his own composition. Since he perceives something unique both within himself and in the world, he no longer has interest in the functionality of the cosmos. Instead, he searches for the reasons behind the world's functionality. He wants to know its origins, its purpose, and

[16] Genesis 2:7–15.
[17] "Lonely Man of Faith," 23.
[18] See the introduction to *Netzah Israel* by Rabbi Judah Loew.

ultimately its Creator,[19] for only then can he know his own reason for being. "In a word, Adam the second explores not the scientific abstract universe but the irresistibly fascinating qualitative world where he establishes an intimate relation with God."[20] His quest for knowledge in intimacy is not influenced by what the other does, but by what the other is.

Because ontological man recognizes through his noesis of the world that he is different from the rest of the world, he realizes that he cannot stand in relation to any other aspect of creation. "And Adam gave names to all the cattle and to the birds of the sky and to all the wild beasts; but Adam did not find a helper opposite him."[21] Recognition of uniqueness, coupled with his inability for self-understanding except via existential association, creates doubt in his sense of being, thus making him lonely. His loneliness stems not from being alone, since epistemological man is also alone as he stresses his own individuality. Its source is in his inability to affirm his own ontology as a being separate from the functional material world. As Rabbi Soloveitchik writes in his article, "Confrontation," about ontological man, "Having been taken out of a state of complacency and optimistic naïveté, he finds the intimate relationship between him and the order of facticity ending in tension and conflict."[22] Loneliness is not a disposition toward being alone but a sense of forlornness or, in Rabbi Soloveitchik's words, it "is nothing but the act of questioning one's own ontological legitimacy, worth, and reasonableness."[23] To remove the sense of loneliness and discover self-awareness and definition through communicable companionship, ontological man must undergo the paradox of cathartic redemptiveness.

Rabbi Soloveitchik defines catharsis, for the purpose of redemption, as a bold move forward toward self-realization by

---

[19] "Lonely Man of Faith," 21.
[20] "Lonely Man of Faith," 23.
[21] Genesis 2:20.
[22] "Confrontation," 13.
[23] "Lonely Man of Faith," 31.

retreating humbly from one's own self.[24] The paradox in his idea of cathartic redemptiveness is twofold. First, for a man who gains knowledge only through subjective experience and relating to the world around him, cathartic redemptiveness occurs within a person without entailing any connection to an externality. As he writes, "Cathartic redemptiveness is experienced in the privacy of one's in-depth personality, and it cuts below the relationship between the 'I' and the 'thou' (to use an existentialist term) and reaches into the very hidden strata of the isolated 'I' who knows himself as a singular being."[25] Moreover, he does not even attempt to engage the world as that newly found "I," focusing instead on his own self-restraint and his retreat from the world. Second, once ontological man becomes able to defeat himself through his own restraint and discovers himself in the depths of his own personality, he recognizes his uniqueness to an even greater extent, which increases his feelings of loneliness. In essence, "each great redemptive step forward in man's quest for humanity entails the ever-growing tragic awareness of his aloneness and only-ness and consequently of his loneliness and insecurity."[26] In order to break this cycle of resignation, he must further restrain himself – yet this time his sacrifice is not in terms of further retreat from the world, but rather a sacrifice of his own being.

Because ontological man sees himself as distinct and alone, any relationship to another ontological man could only occur by virtue of what they distinctly share. Communication through physical language objectifies the experience of being, preventing any true sharing of experience between two lonely individuals. In Rabbi Soloveitchik's words, "Distress and bliss, joys and frustrations are incommunicable within the framework of the natural dialogue consisting of common words. By the time *homo absconditus*[27]

---

[24] "Catharsis," 43.
[25] "Lonely Man of Faith," 35.
[26] "Lonely Man of Faith," 37.
[27] In *Family Redeemed* (21), Rabbi Soloveitchik defines *homo absconditus* as "a 'hidden man' whom no one knows. He hardly knows himself." In *Out of the Whirlwind* (88),

manages to deliver the message, the personal and intimate content of the latter is already recast in the lingual matrix, which standardizes the unique and universalizes the individual."[28] Furthermore, because they are unique vis-à-vis the world and each other by virtue of the introverted catharsis in which they discovered their "I" awareness, "the closer two individuals get to know each other, the more aware they become of the metaphysical distance separating them. Each one exists in a singular manner, completely absorbed in his individual awareness which is egocentric and exclusive."[29] Despite his loneliness and his inability to engage in authentic communication, ontological man still strives to relate to another, since existential relation is the only way in which he can know himself, even if, by seeking communion, he diminishes the recognition of his own uniqueness in the world. It is at this point that the paradox of self-realization occurs. "At this crucial point, if Adam is to bring his quest for redemption to full realization, he must initiate action leading to the discovery of a companion who, even though as unique and singular as he, will master the art of communicating and, with him, form a community."[30] Because what they distinctly share is the divine spirit within them, one ontological man cannot communicate to another ontological man except through their mutual connection with God. Their community, therefore, must entail the divine, which separated ontological man from the material world and caused his loneliness in the first place. God, recognized as the focus of ontological man's search and the only relation with whom he is able to find a means of personal expression, must therefore be ever-present within the redeemed community. Ontological man is able to achieve self-realization as part of the redeemed community because the structure of the

---

he elaborates that even if he is unknown and lacks self-knowledge, he "does not engage in understanding something, nor does he engage in acting out something, but is always concerned with relating to and sharing in something."

28 "Lonely Man of Faith," 67.

29 "Confrontation," 15.

30 "Lonely Man of Faith," 38–39.

redeemed community allows him to maintain his uniqueness while being able to communicate his essence to others, thereby removing his feelings of loneliness.

If ontological man's cathartic redemptiveness does not bring him to a redeemed community governed by Halakha, he can easily fall into the mode of *homo religiosus*. As a man who recognizes his uniqueness in the world, he finds both the world and himself lacking. He sees the world as a mundane place, void of the divinity which he recognizes in himself and which alludes to a holy abode that he cannot enter because of his own physicality. His recognition of divinity gives him a sense of ontic pluralism, in which "[*h*]*omo religiosus* is dissatisfied, unhappy with this world. He searches for an existence that is above empirical reality."[31] He becomes an ascetic, wholly enraptured with God at the expense of the world, a mystic who loses himself in the all-encompassing divinity. In the communion with God, there is nothing else. Where modern man has left no room for his ontological nature, *homo religiosus* has abandoned his epistemological counterpart.

Recognizing that epistemological man and ontological man are only typologies that exist within the man of reality, Rabbi Soloveitchik acknowledges this bifurcation of being and the tension that such a dichotomy in direction towards self-actualization creates.

> The dialectical awareness, the steady oscillating between the majestic natural community and the covenantal faith community renders the act of complete redemption unrealizable. The man of faith, in his continuous movement between the pole of natural majesty and that of covenantal humility, is prevented from totally immersing in the immediate covenantal awareness of the redeeming presence, knowability, and involvement of God in the community of man.[32]

---

[31] *Halakhic Man*, 13.
[32] "Lonely Man of Faith," 80.

The conflict between typologies makes the achievement of dignity impossible as well, for the insecurity of ontological man will never allow epistemological man to be satisfied (as if epistemological man could ever be satisfied) with any value that another assigns to him. Alone in both worlds, man can never fully immerse himself in a community, nor can he succeed in being an authentic individual. In order for man to self-actualize, he must conflate his two typologies into one mode of being that allows him to commune with God and relate to the world both functionally and metaphysically.

God, in revealing Himself to man, gave man the ability to comprehend his meaning and purpose and, through Halakha, provided him with the tools to unify his dichotomous self. Created by Hashem Elohim, the ideal ontological man, as noted by the names of God, is also epistemological, only his epistemic character is subservient to his ontic one. With striking resemblance to the rabbinic description of bifurcated man, ontological man uses his epistemic character to ground himself in the world, to which he relates yet also from which he feels alienated.

> Nehemiah, the son of Rabbi Shmuel son of Nahman, said: 'And it was very good': 'and it was good' refers to the human beings. 'And it was good' refers to the inclination-for-good. 'And it was very good' refers to the evil inclination. But can the evil inclination be considered very good?! In fact, this teaches you that without the evil inclination, a man would not build a house, nor marry a woman, nor father children.[33]

Through Halakha, ontological side of man is able to work together with epistemological side of man for their mutual benefit. In combining his two disparate natures under the rubric of Halakha, man can acknowledge the relationship that he has with God and the world, and his experiential truth is understood in light of the Law. Man achieves an understanding of his essential being and attains

---

[33] *Ecclesiastes Rabbah* 3:11.

dignity by applying Halakha to his life. The person who is able to achieve such a unity of self is the halakhic man.

> Halakhic man is not some illegitimate, unstable hybrid. On the contrary, out of the contradictions and antinomies there emerges a radiant, holy personality whose soul has been purified in the furnace of struggle and opposition and redeemed in the fires of the torments of spiritual disharmony....[34]

It is the halakhic man who exemplifies the ideal for which every man should strive, for he is the only one who understands all aspects of himself, his world, and his relationship with God.

Halakhic man's perception of the world is similar to epistemological man's in methodology, but with one fundamental difference. Both men impose *a priori* laws upon the world; both have their conception of the ideal to which reality is measured. However, where epistemological man's contemplation of reality has no external imposition since it is rooted in his own thought, halakhic man's view of the world carries a moral imperative because its source is God's law.

The view of halakhic man towards the world also resembles epistemological man in its functionality. In order to elucidate, Rabbi Soloveitchik provides the following example:

> When halakhic man comes across a spring bubbling quietly, he already possesses a fixed, a priori relationship with this real phenomenon: the complex laws regarding the halakhic construct of a spring. The spring is fit for the immersion of a *zav* (a man with a discharge); it may serve as *mei hatat* (waters of expiation); it purifies with flowing water; it does not require a fixed quantity of forty se'ahs; etc.[35]

The same is the case with a sunset or sunrise, a clear moonlit night, mighty mountains, or various flora and fauna. All his experiences of the world are measured against an ideal halakhic construct to

---

[34] *Halakhic Man*, 4.
[35] *Halakhic Man*, 20.

determine how to relate to reality. Nothing is seen as itself, only how it can be used within the halakhic paradigm. "He who walks along the path while studying and breaks off his study and says, 'How beautiful is this tree, how beautiful is this fallow field!' Scripture accords it as if he committed a mortal sin."[36] To see the world outside the functionality of Halakha is to misunderstand the world and to remove himself from the community of God.

Although halakhic man shares a methodological approach with epistemological man, his motive is that of ontological man. He desires self-awareness and a cure for his loneliness; in a word, he desires redemption. The difference between ontological and halakhic man is that ontological man does not know how to accomplish his goal. He may easily err and become *homo religiosus* for he does not realize that, as the story in Genesis relates, God imposes His will upon man's self-sacrifice; man does not approach God through his own actions alone. Halakhic man, on the other hand, knows that "[i]f a Jew lives in accordance with Halakha (and a life in accordance with Halakha means, first, the comprehension of Halakha per se and, second, comparing the ideal Halakha and the real world – the act of realization of Halakha), then he shall find redemption."[37] In viewing life through the prism of Halakha, the phenomenology of ontological man is able to become communicable. Although Halakha does not concern itself with metaphysical mysteries but rather is practical and utilitarian[38] and, as such, would suggest that it has no place in ontological man's realm of consciousness, its tendency is to translate the subjective experience into a cognitive, substantive one. The religious act becomes objective and standard, thus allowing universality for the purposes of communication, yet the psychic experience of the religious act remains personal and unique.[39]

---

[36] Mishna *Avot,* 3:8.
[37] *Halakhic Man*, 38.
[38] *Halakhic Man*, 49.
[39] *Halakhic Man*, 57.

For the person who cannot completely internalize Halakha into the essence of his being – or, to paraphrase the words of the Mishna, who is unable to make God's will like his will and nullify his will before God's will – Halakha still has the important function of mitigating man's inner dialectic. While he cannot actualize any aspect of his personality completely, he also cannot abandon any aspect either.

> When man gives himself to the covenantal community the Halakha reminds him that he is also wanted and needed in another community, the cosmic-majestic, and when it comes across man while he is involved in the creative enterprise of the majestic community, it does not let him forget that he is a covenantal being who will never find self-fulfillment outside of the covenant and that God awaits his return to the covenantal community.[40]

Halakha narrows man's inner conflict by inserting elements of one typology into the scope of the other. Ontological man is forced to act within the physical world according to strict equalizing guidelines and epistemological man is forced both to self-reflect and recognize the inherent divinity of his worldly influence. Although man benefits by narrowing his typological vacillation, he remains lonely because he is still not grounded in either community. Only now, it could be argued, his loneliness no longer permeates exclusively in the ontological realm but into the epistemological as well. Since he is not fully immersed in the epistemological community, he will question his legitimacy, worth and reasonableness as a social being, and not only as a unique being.

Modern society has compounded the problem for those who fail to become halakhic men and thus maintain, if only latently, the dialectical schism within their psychology. Because of his focus on technological discovery and advancement for the purpose of material opulence and economic utility, epistemological man has abandoned ontological man and has perverted the ontological

---

40 "Lonely Man of Faith," 82–83.

community from being one of existential self-understanding to one that serves a functional purpose.

> He seeks not the greatness found in sacrificial action but the convenience one discovers in a comfortable, serene state of mind. He is desirous of an aesthetic experience rather than a covenantal one, of a social ethos rather than a divine imperative.[41]

The epistemological side of man has taken away the forum in which the ontological side of man can find expression for his self-awareness, leaving him to remain lonely, his ontic needs repressed in the subconscious of modern man. Assuming that one is able to uncover his ontological self, yet does not have the strength to become a halakhic man, his ontological loneliness is compounded by a communal loneliness that is absent in all other periods of history. While in other eras, man would not have been fully immersed in either community, today, he does not even have a true ontological community to which he can attempt to belong.

Rabbi Soloveitchik's conception of man attempts to provide a foundation for the necessity of Halakha for any realization of being. His focus, however, on man's psychology vis-à-vis the development of religious consciousness and commitment to the religious ideal, seems to emphasize a conception of man qua individual at the expense of also developing an inter-relational conception of man qua active member of society. The implications of this emphasis can be seen in his conception of *tzelem Elohim* (image of God) and dignity (*kavod*), as well as in the description of his respective typologies and the self-actualized halakhic man, in terms of their relationship to the world around them.

Tzelem Elohim (Image of God):

As discussed, Rabbi Soloveitchik describes the image of God as man's inner charismatic endowment as a creative being. The typology created in God's image is interested only in domination

[41] "Lonely Man of Faith," 103.

and using the world for his own benefit. He is attracted by what is beautiful and not by what is good, and his motivation is utilitarian and not in higher moral principles.[42] Even if the society which he creates does live by a certain moral code, its morality is justified only in the economic or pragmatic sense, similar to Immanuel Kant's race of intelligent devils. Rabbi Soloveitchik recognizes the tenuous morality of this person when he writes, "Evidently, civilized men can become the personification of evil. The thin veneer of social restraint can suddenly be lifted, exposing the ugly, brutish potential of man. Created 'in the image of God,' man can also assume a satanic identity. He is capable, from time to time, of going berserk, of turning into a monster."[43] Consistent with the midrash above, the *tzelem Elohim* is perceived to be the evil inclination that must be channeled in a positive, constructive manner.

Because the *tzelem Elohim* is not an innate ideal of which one strives to make manifest in one's life, but rather an inner strength that one must harness through channels external to it, the idea of being created in the image of God is not a source of dignity in and of itself. Rather, it can only help to facilitate its attainment through domination, as we will see below. This is also true with respect to moral action. Rabbi Soloveitchik explains,

> Of course, there is a distinctive element in man, the *Imago Dei*, the *tzelem Elokim*, the image of God. Judaism considered the *imago* element to be not a gratuitous grant bestowed upon man but rather a challenge to be met by man; not as an endowment fashioned by God but rather as a mission to be implemented, as a *hyle*, formless matter to be molded by man. Perhaps the central norm in our ethical system is related to *Imago Dei*, to be like God, reflect His image, become a Divine being, live like a creature who

---

42 "Lonely Man of Faith," 14.

43 *Reflections of the Rav*, 179.

> bears resemblance to its Maker. It is up to man to either realize or shake off the *Imago Dei.*[44]

The meaning of this passage is not that the *tzelem Elohim* itself is the source of man's ethical nature, for Rabbi Soloveitchik continually denies any innate moral sense in this aspect of man's being.[45] Rather, what Rabbi Soloveitchik is affirming is that when man unites the totality of his being, when the image of Elohim is combined with the image of Hashem,[46] his instinct to control the material world will be used to control the microcosm of his own ethical world.

The reason for Rabbi Soloveitchik's definition of *tzelem Elohim* as intrinsically amoral yet endowed with the potential for domination and creative greatness is due to its relationship with the rest of creation. Because man, when he was created in the *tzelem Elohim*, was created in the context of the creation of the natural world, man, in this context, is the pinnacle of creation only in the quantitative sense, and is not qualitatively any different than the world around him. Rabbi Soloveitchik writes, "Human life is evaluated as the apex of the bio-pyramid – what was termed *tzelem* – and plant as its base. But the difference consists only in degree, not in kind."[47] Perceiving man, in his creation in the *tzelem Elohim*, only as the top of the bio-pyramid has two implications. First, man is limited by his natural instinct, just as an animal is limited by its instinct and a plant is limited by its genetic code. There can be no real self-reflection in understanding why one acts, yet his actions can still be quite sophisticated. As Rabbi Soloveitchik explains, "Human personality is motivated and ruled by the instinctive drive, but it attains perfection in the form of technical intelligence which

---

44 *Family Redeemed*, 7.

45 See *The Emergence of Ethical Man,* 76, 144.

46 "The image of *Hashem* is reflected in human longing for the beautiful and noble, in love, in motherly tenderness and fatherly concern, in everything that is great, noble and fascinating in man." (*Family Redeemed*, 9)

47 *The Emergence of Ethical Man,* 43–44.

appoints man as the ruler of other living species."[48] Second, by virtue of the fact that man is the apex of the natural world, he becomes its natural ruler and dominator.[49]

As any image must relate to that which it is represents, the term Elohim must imply the creative aspect of God devoid of a higher sense of morality. Rabbi Soloveitchik defines Elohim as follows: "The term 'Elokim' designates might, force, strength, power, vigor. It designates natural law, and it is for this reason that this term is used in the first story of creation. But in the Torah, the same term also designates a judge; thus God is the source of justice. He is both natural and moral lawgiver."[50] Rabbi Soloveitchik also mentions that the term Elohim connotes God's character of *din* (judgment), since the term can refer either to God or to judges, depending on its context. If Elohim signifies both practical creativity and a sense of judgment, then by this implication, morality must be meant as the principles that maintain the proper functioning of the world, which is consistent with a natural law theory of morality. One could presume that Rabbi Soloveitchik makes a subtle distinction between the two different types of judges in the Jewish tradition where the *dayan*, as it relates to the word *din*, is concerned with maintaining society according to the rules by which it functions, while the *shofet* is concerned with raising the nation's awareness from a naturalistic, mundane focus to one that is directed towards a national relationship with God, as seen in the verse, "When Hashem established *shoftim* for them, Hashem was with the *shofet,* saving them from the hands of their enemies during the *shofet's* life, for Hashem was moved to pity by their outcry before those who oppressed them and who crushed them."[51] I would be wary of such a presumption, however, because it assumes that the immutable particulars of Halakha, as Rabbi Soloveitchik perceives them to be, may at times not produce the ideal society, and it turns *batei din*

---

[48] *The Emergence of Ethical Man,* 73; see also *Abraham's Journey*, 13.

[49] *The Emergence of Ethical Man,* 60.

[50] *Shiurei ha-Rav*, 112.

[51] Judges 2:18.

(courts of judgment) into nothing more than a bureaucratic instrument with as much moral and ethical sway as the Department of Motor Vehicles.

The truth is that Rabbi Soloveitchik does believe in a natural law theory of morality, but the moral aspect of natural law does not stem from the aspect of Elohim. Moral and natural law are the same because of the unity of Hashem and Elohim.[52] In discussing both aspects of God in relation to this idea, he writes, "God [Elohim] is not an ethical personality, whose will is absolute good. Hence the name *Havayah*, 'Lord,' the name that symbolizes God as a personality whose essence and existence are ethically good…"[53] When not joined to the idea of Hashem, Elohim, through the immense power and danger of the natural world, can be seen as cruel. In fact, that is how Rabbi Soloveitchik explains the serpent's perception.

> The experience of God, according to the serpent, is demonic, uncanny, weird. Man should not fear God but should shudder or feel horror before Him. He created man in order to enslave him, to keep him in eternal bondage of incapacity and ineptitude.[54]

If the serpent's perception of God, as One who enjoys His creation by enslaving and dominating it,[55] had any reception in the hearts of men, born in the *tzelem Elohim*, how would this society of natural law look? Rabbi Soloveitchik portrays it through the actions of the *benei ha-elohim*.

> Who were the *benei ha-elohim*? The sons of the privileged few, of the masters, of the robber barons who thought that they were entitled to everything and that no law was

[52] *The Emergence of Ethical Man,* 82.
[53] *The Emergence of Ethical Man,* 98.
[54] *The Emergence of Ethical Man,* 98.
[55] *The Emergence of Ethical Man,* 126.

> applicable to them; men who practiced *hamas* for the sake of enjoying life.[56]

The *benei ha-elohim* resembled their God as the natural and moral lawgiver, albeit without relation to Hashem,[57] in being powerful, egocentric and ego-enjoying. One must wonder, though, if the *benei ha-elohim* were called as such, not according to their actions, but according to their responsibilities. In other words, were they called *benei ha-elohim* because of their actions or despite of them?

The term *tzelem Elohim* occurs twice in the Bible. The first instance, which discusses the creation of man, is the starting point for Rabbi Soloveitchik's theory of the epistemological typology and the source of his definition for *tzelem Elohim* as man's specific charisma and the source of his creative powers. However, the second time the term is mentioned reveals a certain moral statement: "Whoever sheds man's blood, by man shall his blood be shed; for in the image of God made He man. And you, be fruitful, and multiply; swarm in the earth, and multiply therein."[58] This instruction is given to Noah after the Deluge. If we notice carefully, God blessed Noah and instructed him to procreate at the beginning and at the end of the prophecy, the middle of which discusses the permissibility of killing animals for food and the prohibition against murder. In the prophecy to Adam, on the other hand, God blessed him and commanded him to procreate and afterwards informed him of his position of limited domination, restricted by his inability to kill animals for food. He did not repeat to Adam the blessing to procreate as He did with Noah. The necessity to emphasize life and procreation with Noah and not with Adam is due to Noah's permission to take the lives of animals. The *tzelem Elohim* of both Adam and Noah alludes to the responsibility of man over the lives of others due to his exalted position.[59] His dominion over the world

---

[56] *The Emergence of Ethical Man,* 126.
[57] By the time of Enosh, man's relationship to *Hashem* became distanced.
[58] Genesis 9:6–7.
[59] See ibn Ezra's commentary Genesis 1:26, where he references the Gaon.

obligates him to protect it, as implied by the Talmudic statement, "He who acquires a slave acquires a master."[60] Even if a person does not honor himself, he must honor others who are also created in the *tzelem Elohim*,[61] for if one must respect that which he must protect, how much more must he respect his equal.

One who murders another is considered as if he has destroyed the whole world.[62] In committing such an act, he has failed in his responsibility as one created in the *tzelem Elohim*. It becomes the responsibility of others, who have also been created in the *tzelem Elohim*, to protect the rest of the world, which is now threatened by the murderer. The emphasis on the last clause of God's warning against murder is not on the one who has been murdered. Rather, it is up to man in general to protect that for which he is responsible.

It cannot be argued that the admonition to not murder because man is made in the *tzelem Elohim* is from the perspective of natural and not moral law. This can be seen in the double warning against murder made in this passage:

> Every moving thing that lives shall be yours for food; like the green herbage I have given you everything. But flesh; with its soul its blood you shall not eat. However, your blood which belongs to your souls I will demand, of every beast will I demand it; but of man, of every man for that of his brother I will demand the soul of man. Whoever sheds man's blood, by man shall his blood be shed; for in the image of God made He man. And you, be fruitful, and multiply; swarm in the earth, and multiply therein.[63]

God first warns against retribution for the killing of a human being, directing the statement towards both man and animals. Only after does He warn man against killing another and provides a reason for such, namely that man has a certain innate quality. Nahmanides, in relation to equating man and animals in desert for retribution,

---

60 BT *Kiddushin* 20a.

61 *Sefer Mitzvot Katan*, Commandment 8.

62 Mishna *Sanhedrin* 4:5.

63 Genesis 9:3–7.

comments that animals do not have [moral] intelligence to be deserving of punishment or reward, and he resigns to understanding the warning as a divine decree. The repetition in the text could be seen as the superposing of moral law onto natural law. Rashi explains the expression, "of every beast," as necessary because, "since the generation of the flood sinned, and they were cast loose to be food for evil beasts [and for the beasts] to rule over them…therefore [the Torah] needed to enjoin the beasts regarding killing them." If, then, the first sentence prohibits both man and animals from killing man, thereby restoring natural law which needs no other reason than divine decree, would not the second sentence, which gives a reason from which we learn about ourselves and others, provide a moral connotation? Because the reason the second sentence gives is that man is created in the *tzelem Elohim*, it must have moral significance per se.

How can we account for the *tzelem Elohim* that makes man both exalted and morally responsible for the world in which he lives? Or, to put it differently, how can we broaden our understanding of the meaning of Elohim, in the image of which we are created? The first of the Ten Commandments states, "I am Hashem, your Elohim, who took you out of the land of Egypt, out of the house of bondage. You shall not have other Elohim in My presence."[64] Because Hashem overrode the laws of nature and miraculously took Israel out of the land of Egypt, He is known to them as Elohim.[65] The causal relationship is more clearly demonstrated by the verse, "I am Hashem your Elohim, who took you out of the land of Egypt to be an Elohim to you; I am Hashem your Elohim."[66] God took a providential role with Israel and chose Israel to be His special nation; therefore, Israel has a responsibility to serve Him. There is an intimate, personal connection between master and servant. For this reason, Israel is commanded not to have any other Elohim in

---

[64] Exodus 20:2.
[65] See Rashi's commentary on Exodus 20:2.
[66] Numbers 15:41.

His presence. Elohim does not describe a transcendent God who is absent from everyday life; rather it describes an immanent God who is forever present in the lives of the people.

The idea that Elohim implies an immanent God is portrayed in the episode between Elijah and the prophets of Baal. Elijah, rebuking the people for their wavering between serving God and worshipping idols, says to them, "How long will you keep hopping between two opinions? If Hashem is Elohim, follow Him, and if Baal, follow him!"[67] Rabbi Solomon ben Aderet, explains the curious rebuke as follows:

> Know that the prophets of Baal, with their foolishness, were not foolish in the idea that the Creator, blessed be He, is the cause of all and that everything comes from Him, who is Blessed. Rather, they thought His greatness precluded Him from divine providence…And they thought that He, who is Blessed, gave His world chiefs who run the world and made them masters of the world….[68]

While the Jews recognized Hashem as the transcendent Creator of the world, they vacillated in the idea that a transcendent Creator could also be an immanent ruler. In Elijah's words, they questioned whether Hashem could be Elohim, demonstrating once more that the name Elohim implies a personal God who cares about his people. Through his challenge against the prophets of Baal, Elijah was able to prove a principal tenet of the Jewish faith, "Hear, Israel: Hashem is our Elohim, Hashem is one."[69] This is not a tautology that God is God and, as God, He is one. Rather, it is the idea that the God of transcendence is the same as the God of immanence. There is only one God, who both created the world and continually maintains it through divine providence.[70] It now becomes apparent why only the name Elohim is necessary in the first chapter of

---

[67] I Kings 18:21.
[68] Rashba, *Hiddushei ha-Aggadot*, *Berakhot* 6b.
[69] Deuteronomy 6:4.
[70] *Man and God*, 29.

Genesis. It is obvious that Hashem, as the transcendent aspect of God, is involved in creation. To know that Elohim, the personal, providential aspect of God, is involved in creation is innovative.

This idea is further corroborated by Nahmanides's understanding of the relationship between God's aspects as Hashem and Elohim. Nahmanides, like Rabbi Judah Halevi, defines Elohim as "the Master of all forces" or "the Force of all forces,"[71] yet on the first of the Ten Commandments, regarding the phrase, "*Anokhi Hashem Elohekha*," he writes, "He said, I am Hashem your Elohim, thus teaching and commanding that they should know that Hashem exists and He is Elohim to them. That is to say, there exists an Eternal being through Whom everything has come into existence by His will and power, and He is Elohim to them, who are obligated to worship Him." This seems to me to imply that Hashem is unknowable except through being known as Hashem Elohim, where the transcendent, unknowable and Eternal being is also the Creator and Preserver of the world with whom Israel has a relationship as Elohim.

It is important to emphasize that it is not that Elohim is a personal God and Hashem is an impersonal God; rather, God is a personal God and one can only encounter this personal God when He is manifest as Hashem Elohim, since Hashem per se is unknowable. In his commentary, Rabbi Samson Raphael Hirsch writes the following about the relationship between the name Hashem and Elohim,

> In *Shema Yisrael* God is called *Eloheinu*, it is God as He proclaims Himself *Hashem* to the nation. *Ve-Ahavta* turns to each individual and shows God to him as 'his' God, *Hashem Elohekha* how He looks after him individually in the whole course of his life and would guide him in all his actions. Every individual person is a special object of God's love and guidance and it is just as 'your' God that you have to

[71] Commentary on Genesis 1:3.

> think of Him, what He was and is and will be to 'you' if you truly conceive love for Him.[72]

Similarly, just as one cannot encounter the aspect of Hashem without the aspect of Elohim conjoined to it, so too can one not encounter the aspect of Elohim without the aspect of Hashem as a silent partner. Because there is only one God and different names are only necessary due to our inability to unify our different perceptions of Him, the different uses of Hashem, Hashem Elohim, and Elohim in the Bible connote different levels of our perception of God's relatedness to the world, both in terms of how we sense His presence and in how we explain the manner in which events occur.

For example, it is well accepted that the aspect of Elohim is related to judgment (*midat ha-din*) and Hashem to mercy (*midat ha-rahamim*). However, God's attribute of judgment is not anything like a strict justice that has no room for pardon and compassion.[73] This can be exemplified in two different forms of execution of God's judgment – the manner in which God judges man and the manner in which God's Law demands that a Jewish court judge man. Maimonides, basing himself on two Talmudic passages,[74] writes regarding man's judgment,

---

[72] *The Pentateuch: Deuteronomy*, 92.

[73] *Abraham's Journey*, 70.

[74] The first, *Rosh Hashana* 17a, states, "In the school of Rabbi Ishmael they taught, 'He puts aside every first iniquity; and herein lies the attribute.' Raba said, 'The iniquity itself is not obliterated, and if there is an excess of iniquities [God] reckons it with the others.'" The second passage, in Yoma 86b, states, "Rabbi Yosi bar Judah said: If a man commits a transgression, the first, second and third time he is forgiven, the fourth time he is not forgiven, as it is said, 'Thus says the Lord, for three transgressions of Israel, yea for four, I will not reverse it,' and furthermore it says, 'Lo, all these things does God work, twice, yea, three times, with a man.' What does 'furthermore it say' serve for? One might have assumed that applies only to a community, but not to an individual; therefore, come and hear [the additional verse], 'Lo, all these things does God work, twice, yea, three times with a man.'"

> When a person's sins are being weighed against his merits, [God] does not count a sin that was committed only once or twice. [A sin] is only [counted] if it was committed three times or more. Should it be found that [even] those sins committed more than three times outweigh a person's merits, the sins that were committed twice [or less] are also added and he is judged for all of his sins. If his merits are equal to [or greater than the amount of] his sins committed which were committed more than three times, [God] forgives his sins one after the other, i.e. the third sin [is forgiven because] it is considered his first sin, for the two previous sins were already forgiven. Similarly, after the third sin is forgiven, the fourth sin is considered as a 'first' [sin and is forgiven according to the same principle]. The same [pattern is continued] until [all his sins] are concluded.[75]

The second example is regarding the deliberation of the court in a case involving capital punishment. During deliberation a judge who had first proposed a rationale for exoneration cannot then propose a rationale for conviction.[76] If one of the students who sit in observation of the court proceedings declares that he has a rationale for conviction, he is silenced, yet if he has a rationale for exoneration, he is brought in to participate in the deliberations. Even the defendant himself can proffer arguments in his defense.[77] The principle that the court is permitted to hear any view in favor of the accused, but not any view against him, tells of a judicial perspective that is based on more than just the natural laws of cause and effect. The *midat ha-din* of Elohim, whether it be manifest in divine judgment or divinely inspired human judgment, has instilled within it a compassionate approach. The difference in the

---

[75] *Hilkhot Teshuva* 3:5. There is a difference between the judgment of an individual and of a community since community sins are held in abeyance until final reckoning.

[76] *Hilkhot Sanhedrin* 10:2.

[77] *Hilkhot Sanhedrin* 10:8.

compassion in *midat ha-din* and the mercy of *midat ha-rahamim*, however, is not one of degree. As the root of the word *rahamim* insinuates, the mercy of the aspect of Hashem is not embedded within the laws of the world as with Elohim. Rather, like the womb that surrounds the fetus, nourishing it while at the same time wholly separate from it, the *midat ha-rahamim* is a supernatural influence stemming from a transcendental source.

Rabbi Soloveitchik maintains that he derives his notion of Elohim as divine cosmic dynamics and Hashem as the transcendent yet personal characteristic of God from Rabbi Judah Halevi.[78] If one examines the discussion of God's names in *The Kuzari*, however, it becomes apparent that it does not support Rabbi Soloveitchik's distinction. Rabbi Judah Halevi does intimate that the characteristic of Elohim can be grasped through cognition, and as such could be associated with epistemological man, and that Hashem cannot be understood through speculation but only by intuition. As the king of the Khazars understands, "Man yearns for Hashem as a matter of love, taste, and conviction; while attachment to Elohim is the result of speculation."[79]

Yet when one understands the words of the rabbi, the notion of Hashem and Elohim are not as the king expresses. In describing the mistake of idolatry among the nations, the rabbi asserts that the nations recognized the existence of a transcendent God but saw no use to serve Him since His exaltedness precluded any possibility for Him to have any knowledge or care for the individual. Therefore, the nations' worship consisted of serving intermediaries, which they named Elohim.[80] For Jews, who recognize no divine liaisons, Hashem is the personal name of God.[81] The personal relatedness stems from the fact that the Jews recognize that Hashem relates to them in the same manner as the nations think their Elohim do,

---

[78] "Lonely Man of Faith," 51.

[79] *The Kuzari*, 223.

[80] *The Kuzari*, 198–199.

[81] *The Kuzari*, 201.

which means that Hashem is both transcendent and immanent at the same time. The rabbi explains, "The God of this [pure] essence is only and solely Hashem, and because He established a connection with man, the name Elohim was altered after the creation into Hashem Elohim. This the sages express in the words: A 'full name over a full universe.'"[82] Contrary to Rabbi Soloveitchik, man does not relate to Hashem intuitively and Elohim cognitively. It is impossible to understand Hashem, as the essence of God; one can only know God through how He acts and relates to the world, which is the characteristic of Elohim. If Elohim implies the ability for transcendent Hashem to relate to the Jews as a personal God, Elohim cannot solely be cognitively recognized as divine cosmic dynamics; it must connote a characteristic that allows connection, where "the finite 'I' meets the infinite He 'face-to-face.'"[83] Elohim is the only way through which man can know Hashem, albeit as Hashem Elohim, and as such, Elohim must entail care and responsibility. It is for this reason that the rabbi introduces his belief to the king of Khazars with the response that he believes in the Elohim of Abraham, Isaac and Israel, who led the Jews out of Egypt.[84] Hashem, the transcendent God, is Elohim, the immanent God who cares and is responsible for His people.

Maimonides defines the term *tzelem* as applying "to the notion in virtue of which a thing is constituted as a substance and becomes what it is. It is the true reality of the thing in so far as the latter is that particular being. In man that notion is that from which human apprehension derives. It is on account of this intellectual apprehension that it is said of man: *In the image of God created He him*."[85] Therefore, the *tzelem Elohim* of which man is comprised can not only be an egocentric potential which man must harness in his psychological transformation from a natural to a religio-ethical being but must also inherently entail a moral relationship between

[82] *The Kuzari*, 220.
[83] "Lonely Man of Faith," 51.
[84] *The Kuzari*, 44.
[85] *Guide for the Perplexed*, 22

man and the rest of creation that demands an intimate and personal concern with the world. Man must see it in terms of his self-definition qua independent individual and as a member of a community. It promotes mastery and domination, but not of pure functionality and utilitarianism. It is a *noblesse oblige.*

Dignity *(Kavod)*

Quoting the words of the Psalmist, "For you made him a little lower than the angels and have crowned him with glory and honor (dignity),"[86] Rabbi Soloveitchik equates being human to living with dignity. Dignity, as he interprets the verse, means man's capability of dominating his environment and exercising control over it; dignity is a consequence of glory and not something in addition to it.[87] Elsewhere he gives further description.

> We may formulate the following equation: to be created in the image of God = to be endowed with dignity = to be capable of finding God and communing with Him – and to commune with God is the greatest victory on the part of man. In conclusion: the dignity of man and his divine character assert themselves in triumph and conquest.[88]

Rabbi Soloveitchik does not mean in this sense a finding and communing with God in terms of how man perceives his relationship with the divine but in how that relationship influences man's relationship to the world around him. He explains,

> Questing for God is synonymous with surging forward and reaching out eagerly for anchorage and security. The human being who is driven and pressed for creative heroic action – who aims at the enlargement of self by conquering and subduing whatever sectors of being lie outside his small world – moves towards God. In Him he finds freedom from insecurity and fear, which is a *conditio sine qua non* for

[86] Psalms 8:6.
[87] "Lonely Man of Faith," 15.
[88] *Out of the Whirlwind*, 107.

> man to conquer the world, to develop his ability, to realize and fulfill himself. He finds self-assertion, boundless self-expansion, and serenity.[89]

Because glory, a distinction accorded by common consent and, therefore, an externally produced sense of value, engenders dignity, which is only asserted in the externality of conquest, a person's self-respect is only a reflection of what others think of him.

In translating the word, *kavod*, in terms of both honor and dignity, Rabbi Soloveitchik is implying that the words have the same meaning in the Jewish tradition. A person's honor is his dignity by the simple transitive property; his *kavod*, which translates to his honor, is his *kavod*, which translates to his dignity. Because we commonly use the expression of giving honor to someone, it is a popular misconception that honor, and hence dignity, is an externally imposed quality. It is true that both honor and dignity are closely related, and hence can be defined by the same word, yet dignity can not be a consequence of the honor that others bestow. Rather, honor must be the external manifestation of the internal quality of dignity.

The idea that *kavod* can be used when referring to the essence of something is demonstrated in a discussion between God and Moses. After God accepts Moses's entreaty on behalf of Israel that He, Himself, should lead them through the desert, Moses asks, "Oh, show me Your *kavod*!" God responds that He will show Moses His actions of goodness and compassion, but Moses cannot see God Himself, "for no man can see Me and live."[90] Although Moses wanted to understand God's essence, not only His attributes, he used the word *kavod* to convey his desire. It is apparent that *kavod* in this context is not what Moses was giving to God, nor is it an awareness of God's action in order for Moses to bestow honor. Rather, it signifies an internal quality that Moses wanted to

---

[89] *Out of the Whirlwind*, 106.
[90] Exodus 33:17–23.

comprehend. Maimonides explains the idea of *kavod* as it pertains to this passage as follows:

> The expression [*kavod*] is sometimes intended to signify His essence and true reality, may He be exalted, as when he says, *Show me, I pray Thee, Thy glory*, and was answered: *For man shall not see Me and live.* This answer indicates that the *glory* that is spoken of here is His essence, and the [Moses'] saying *Thy glory* is by way of honoring Him…For the true way of honoring Him consists in apprehending His greatness. Thus everybody who apprehends His greatness and His perfection honors Him according to the extent of his apprehension.[91]

In this sense, no one can ever give *kavod* to another; giving *kavod* is really only giving recognition to the dignity that the person already has.

The idea of *kavod* as an internal quality is further developed by the sages in the Mishna, who state that the person who gives *kavod* to others is the one who truly has it.[92] If *kavod* were an externally produced quality, then the person with *kavod* should be the one who receives it and not the one who gives it, since it cannot be that honoring others means dominating or imposing oneself upon them. Moreover, if one looks at the other examples of the Mishna, it becomes clear that *kavod* stems from an internal sense of self-esteem. I will quote it in its entirety.

> Ben Zoma would say: Who is wise? One who learns from every man, as is stated, 'From all my teachers I have grown wise, for Your testimonials are my meditation.' Who is strong? One who overpowers his inclinations, as is stated, 'Better one who is slow to anger than one with might, one who rules his spirit than the captor of a city.' Who is rich? One who is satisfied with his lot, as is stated, 'If you eat of the toil of your hands, fortunate are you, and good is to

[91] *Guide for the Perplexed*, 156–157.

[92] Mishna *Avot* 4:1.

> you'; 'fortunate are you' in this world, 'and good is to you' in the World to Come. Who is honorable? One who honors his fellows, as is stated, 'For to those who honor me, I accord honor; those who scorn me shall be demeaned.'

If ben Zoma defined these four characteristics together, it is only because he perceived a relationship between them. The wise person is not a person who can demonstrate to others an incredible mass of knowledge; rather, it is someone who is so confident in his own knowledge that he is not afraid to learn another perspective from someone else. He is able to respect others' ideas because he does not see them as a threat to his own. Similarly, a strong person is not one who dominates others. He does not need to demonstrate his strength to the public in order to receive recognition. He controls his emotions, spirit, and inclinations, and is able to understand his own boundaries. It is strength of character and not of muscle. The rich man also is not one who feels the need to live lavishly. One who measures his wealth by his possessions thinks, "Since a richer man is a more successful man, why should I cut short my success?" The one who is happy with his lot need not prove himself by what possessions he owns. His possessions assist him in living his life. They do not define it.

All three characteristics portray the relationship of a self-assured person to the outside world. Dignity and honor should be seen in the same light. One who has dignity can honor someone else without feeling that he has sacrificed his own sense of worth. Dignity is not something someone else can give, and neither is honor for that matter. The dignified person recognizes his own true value and, thanks to his self-esteem, can recognize the value of others.

Ambiguity in the relationship between dignity and honor can lead to a seeming contradiction between the words of ben Zoma and the statement of Rabbi Eleazar HaKappar who states, "Jealousy, lust, and *kavod* remove a man from the world."[93] How

[93] Mishna *Avot* 4:28.

can *kavod*, which is the manifestation of an inner dignified essence, remove a man from the world? Yet, when seen in relationship to the other sources of excision stated by Rabbi Eleazar, it becomes obvious that it is not the outwardly-focused internality of a person, i.e. his dignity, that removes him from the world, but rather when he reverses his perspective inwardly to focus on his own self worth vis-à-vis the world around him, i.e. his honor, does he risk his place within it.

Like the word *"kavod,"* the Hebrew root for the word "jealousy" has a double entendre based upon perspective. Jealousy (קנאה), which is a passion aroused over an anticipated perceived loss that a person values, is related to zealotry (קנאות), which also arouses comparable passion when the zealot feels that something he values is at stake. The fundamental difference is whether the value to which the person is devoted is internal or external to himself. The jealous man is passionately dedicated to his own self interest; the zealot to an ideal. Because they were jealous of Moses and Aaron, "the earth opened and swallowed up Dathan, and covered the company of Abiram."[94] On the other hand, Pinchas, who killed Zimri and Salu because he was zealous for God, received a covenant of peace[95] and, as Elijah, will herald the coming of the Messiah. Only in reference to God can jealousy and zeal be identical, since, in His absolute unity, there can be no subjectivity within the conflation of His will and His wisdom. Similarly, the difference between desire and lust is that the latter is a more self-centered, destructive version of the former. For example, Jews are permitted to eat as much meat as they desire (בכל אות נפשך), yet in the desert when the mixed multitude lusted after meat even though they were offered divine sustenance in the form of manna, they were killed by their lust in Kivrot HaTaavah. In both cases, the change of focus from implementing God's will in the world to improving one's own position in the world at the expense of God's

---

94 Psalms 106:17.

95 Numbers 25:11–15.

will forfeits all that one hopes to achieve. So too, focusing on increasing one's own honor, as opposed to recognizing that all that God created was for His honor,[96] will remove a man from the world.

Thought versus Action

Regarding Rabbi Soloveitchik's conception of man in general, the first thing one may notice is that all typologies of man in his thought are described solely in terms of their intellectual outlook vis-à-vis the world. The physical manifestation of each typology's perspective, which is only an irrelevant consequence of its intellect, has no value in and of itself. For example, epistemological man's true ideal is the creation of mathematical constructs that can duplicate the functional relationships existing in the world, while *homo religiosus* leaves the physical world altogether. Even halakhic man has no inherent relationship to the real world, since his focus of concern is the ideal world of Halakha.[97] For example, Rabbi Soloveitchik reinterprets the idea that preference is towards study if and only if that study will generate action[98] as follows:

> The maxim of the sages, 'Great is study, for it leads to action,' has a twofold meaning: 1) action may mean determining the Halakha or ideal norm; 2) action may refer to implementing the ideal norm in the real world. Halakhic man stresses action in its first meaning.[99]

This innovative interpretation removes all importance from the realm of action. The traditional interpretation, however, emphasizes the importance of action in the halakhic world. Based on the above passage and the passage relating to King Hezekiah's funeral,[100] the Tosafists write that action takes precedence over one's own study;

---

96 Mishna *Avot* 6:11.
97 *Halakhic Man*, 24.
98 BT *Kiddushin* 40b.
99 *Halakhic Man*, 64.
100 BT *Bava Kama* 17a.

yet teaching others takes precedence over action. If one has not yet learned how to act, he is not able to do so, while if he has already learned the right way to act, such action takes priority over further study.[101] On the other hand, teaching takes precedence over everything, though only because through teaching more people will know the right way to act, and the collective amount of right action will be maximized.

The idea that Torah study is preparation for action is also evident in the Talmudic discussion between two students who were analyzing contradictory verses. They concluded that if a commandment cannot be performed by someone else, then one should do it oneself even if by doing so, one gives up the opportunity to perform an even greater mitzvah. However, if someone else can perform the commandment, then one should give precedence to the commandment that is considered to be greater. They continue that if a mitzvah must be performed and it can be done by someone else, then one should not interrupt his study in order to perform it. If it cannot be performed by someone else, then one should interrupt his study.[102] Obviously, we must consider the parallel between the greater commandment and studying Torah when we analyze the two imperatives. The greater commandment and, by analogy, studying Torah, is only considered greater in the eyes of the one performing it. A person cannot know objectively which commandments are greater, as evidenced by the Torah's granting of the same reward for honoring one's parents as for sending away a mother bird before taking her eggs from the nest. Only the gravity of a prohibition can be measured because each prohibition has a corresponding punishment associated with it.

The difference between the first statement and the second is that, contrary to what is found in the former, while the person is studying Torah, he is already involved in performing a commandment, and there is a concept in Halakha which states that

[101] Tosafot, *Kiddushin* 40b.
[102] BT *Moed Katan* 9a–b.

one who is performing a commandment is exempt from performing any others during that time. Yet the students declare that he must stop performing the commandment with which he is presently engaged in order to perform a different one that he deems of lesser value![103] The reason for the exception to the general principle that one who is occupied with performing a commandment is exempt from all others is that while studying Torah is important in itself, it is not an end in itself. The Torah was given to human beings rather than the angels because human beings live in the world and experience the actual problems that the Torah addresses. Torah study is preparation for acting according to the Torah's principles, and when the time comes for a person to apply all that he has learned, he is the only one who can realize his own potential. No one else can do so in his stead.

The assertion of the primacy of action developed in the medieval period both in terms of shaping one's perspective on the proper manner of study and in terms of depicting self-perfection. In his book, *Sefer Hasidim*, Rabbi Judah HaHasid equates learning Torah for the purpose of proper action as studying Torah *lishma.* He writes,

> The root of Torah is that man needs to delve into and study and know [the proper performance of commanded] actions completely, as it is stated, 'Good understanding to all their practitioners.' It does not say to their investigators, rather to their practitioners so that a person should not read and learn and kick his father or teacher or someone greater than he. Rather, he should learn in order to teach, to protect, and to perform, and that is [called] Torah *lishma*, and [regarding] everyone who engages in Torah but not *lishma*, it would have been better had they not been born. And everyone who delves into the Torah and knows the commandments

103 Maimonides rules that this is the Halakha. See *Hilkhot Talmud Torah* 3:4.

> but does not perform them, whoa to him and his *mazal*, since he will toil in this world [only] to inherit *Gehenom*.[104]
>
> If a man wishes to study *lishma*, what shall he intend in his heart when he studies? [He should think that] all that I will study, I will practice.[105]

Intellectual excellence alone will not allow a person to develop a relationship with God; in fact, knowledge that is not put into action is detrimental to the person, as it causes him to inherit *Gehenom*. Learning creates greater consequences for man's action and inaction; therefore, the intention of one's learning must be towards it final implementation in performance of the commandments.

The author of *Orhot Tzaddikim* gives greater recognition to study itself than does Rabbi Judah HaHasid, yet he does not disagree as to the proper intention, and thus the final purpose, of Torah study. He writes,

> There is none among the mitzvot that equals Torah study; to the contrary, Torah study equals all the mitzvot, for it leads to their performance. The sages dictum, 'Torah study is opposite all of them,' applies to the one who studies in order to learn, teach, observe, do, and fulfill, and who, because of his set time for Torah study, cannot fulfill all of the mitzvot, but who, when he is not learning, does all that he can, thereby demonstrating his desire to perform all the mitzvot. In his case Torah study is over and above all, for when he studies the mitzva and desires to fulfill it, he is rewarded as if he has fulfilled it, his set time for Torah study having prevented him from doing so in deed. The result is that he receives reward for both doing and studying. But if one is given to idling at times when he could have been performing a mitzva, not caring to perform it, or if when he performs a mitzva he is not

---

104 Siman 17.

105 Siman 944.

> sufficiently heedful of its details, with respect to him it is not stated, 'Torah study is opposite all of them.'[106]

Torah study allows for the consideration that "to study about a command is as if to perform it," yet not without the stipulation that the reason for failure to perform is an external circumstance and not an internal motivation. What is important is the act itself; study only replaces the act as a secondary measure. Ideally, however, study, while important in itself, is not an end in itself but rather preparation for practice.

Some have put forward that books read by the general populace[107] and written for the sake of advancing a universal ethic for a community would naturally promote action over study as a religious priority. Elitist religious scholars, on the other hand, would favor intellectual achievement over practical performance. Rabbi Norman Lamm, for example, argues that Maimonides, in his *Guide for the Perplexed*, advances the opinion that the intellectualization of Torah is greater than its practice, i.e. the Torah is the greatest good and the performance of the commandments is secondary. He supports his contention with Maimonides's description, in the concluding chapter of the *Guide*, of the highest form of man's perfection. Maimonides writes,

> The fourth kind of perfection is the true perfection of man; the possession of the highest intellectual faculties; the possession of such notions which lead to true metaphysical opinions as regards God. With this perfection man has obtained his final object; it gives him true human perfection; it remains to him alone; it gives him immortality, and on its account he is called man. [108]

---

106 Sha'ar Torah

107 There is a debate among scholars if *Sefer Hasidim* was intended for an elite or a general audience. *Orhot Tzaddikim* was designed to be a very popular code of ethics.

108 *Torah Lishma*, 143. Rabbi Lamm uses the Friedlander translation; quote found on page 395.

Considering that man becomes fully perfect through the refinement of his intellectual faculties and moral perfection takes a subordinate position, it would seem that Maimonides would agree with Rabbi Akiva that Talmud Torah is greater than action. However, when one examines the final passage in the *Guide*, which discusses the way of life of a perfect person, it becomes more apparent that Maimonides remains in line with the exclamation of the sages. Maimonides asserts that true worship is to have one's heart constantly filled with longing after God, which is only possible when the intellect is perfected since man's love for God is identical with his knowledge of Him. The manner in which one lives while continually meditating on the Creator, however, is not through pure speculation. He writes, "The way of life of such an individual, after he has achieved this apprehension, will always have in view *loving-kindness*, *righteousness*, and *judgment*, through assimilation to His actions, may He be exalted…"[109] Elsewhere, he equates Talmud Torah with the performance of the commandments as a way toward communion with God, implying that it serves as a fulfillment of a commandment, on par with every other, and not an institution in and of itself.[110] The manner in which the perfect individual lives demonstrates that although Talmud Torah is of primary importance for the intellectual perfection of man, once perfect, his actions are of supreme importance, as they are a natural result of his communing with God.

This idea is supported in Maimonides's other writings. In *Hilkhot Deot*, he writes, "A person should direct his heart and the totality of his behavior to one goal, becoming aware of God,

---

[109] *Guide for the Perplexed*, 638.

[110] *Guide for the Perplexed*, 622. Maimonides does articulate that Talmud Torah and performance of commandments are not equal with respect to acquiring knowledge of God. While performance of the commandments invokes fear of God, Talmud Torah invokes love of God. (*Guide*, 630)

blessed be He."[111] While it is true that in the *Shemonah Perakim* Maimonides promotes the study of medicine as among the greatest acts of worship,[112] the man who actually carries out continual awareness of God is described as follows: "I refer to a man…who does not perform an important or trivial action nor utter a word unless that action or that word leads to virtue or to something leading to virtue; and who reflects and deliberates upon every action and motion, sees whether it leads to that goal or not, and then does it."[113] This is a person who is not engaged solely in speculation of the divine; rather, consideration of the divine is manifest in the performance of every action, as Maimonides supports this position with the rabbinic adage, "Let all your deeds be for the sake of Heaven."[114] Understanding that for Maimonides, study is axiologically prior to deed, not in the traditional sense where one must study how to act in order to act properly but rather in the sense that study will lead a person to self-perfection whereby all his actions will then be focused towards communion with God, one is able to understand the relationship between study and action in the *Mishneh Torah.* Maimonides writes that if one's father does not arrange for his education, he must arrange for it himself, using the proof-text, "And you shall study them and take heed to perform them." He then concludes, "Similarly, in every place, one finds that study takes precedence over action, for study brings about action, but action does not bring about study."[115] When dealing with the initiation of study, Maimonides stresses the importance of study itself, yet study still takes precedence over proper action because it is its cause. However, by adding his original expression, "but action does not bring about study," Maimonides alludes to much more than just the proper fulfillment of commandments. This idea is further supported by his repetition where he writes, "None of the

[111] *Hilkhot Deot* 3:2 .
[112] *Ethical Writings of Maimonides*, 75.
[113] *Ethical Writings of Maimonides*, 77–78.
[114] Mishna *Avot* 2:15.
[115] *Hilkhot Talmud Torah* 1:3.

other mitzvot can be equated to the study of Torah. Rather, the study of Torah can be equated to all the mitzvot, because study leads to action. Therefore, study takes precedence over action in all cases."[116] Could this law not be read as a summary of the end of the *Guide* in stating that study, which will lead a person to the highest level of perfection, i.e. intellectual perfection, is preferred over the fulfillment of the commandments without first attaining intellectual perfection, thereby being the source for the attainment of the subordinate level moral perfection, because only when one attains intellectual perfection can he properly worship God through his actions? If so, it becomes understandable that one should study Torah even if not *lishma* since the intellectual refinement will cause one to begin to study *lishma*, since only according to one's intellectual refinement can one's deeds be measured.[117]

Where Maimonides saw action as the final end and a consequence of self-perfection, Rabbi Hasdai Crescas understood action to be its impetus, thereby returning to the ideas of the *Hasidei Ashkenaz* that study is essential in that it allows for proper action. He writes,

> …when His Hesed, may He be blessed, decreed to make us, the congregation of Israel, *shlemim*, he increased for us [commanded] actions, as the saying of Rabbi Hanina ben Akashia, 'The Holy One, blessed be He, desired to credit Israel; therefore He increased upon them Torah and mitzvot.' The performance of the mitzvot brings *shlemut*, and the performance is impossible without knowledge of [its particulars], and this is the simple [understanding] of the matter in the Mishna, 'Talmud Torah is opposite all of them.' This is how they voted and taught, that Talmud is *ikar*, since it will lead to action.[118]

---

116 *Hilkhot Talmud Torah* 3:3.
117 *Hilkhot Talmud Torah* 3:5.
118 *Or Hashem*, Preface.

According to Rabbi Crescas, God gave Israel the means for perfection through increasing the amount of commandments and the Torah to instruct how to fulfill them, implying that the more commandments one fulfills the more perfect one may be able to become. Man's intellectual development, unlike in Maimonides's conception, seemingly has no independent role in the development of an individual; its benefit derives from its implementation.

Towards the end of the early modern period, the balance of priority between study and practice began to shift. Rabbi Hayyim of Volozhin considered constant, uninterrupted study of Torah to be the ideal, even deeming study itself as an act of communion with the divine. Study is considered preferable to action to the point that Rabbi Hayyim asserts that even study that is not done *lishma* is preferred over performance of the commandments that is done *lishma*. However, as resolute as Rabbi Hayyim is that continual study of Torah is of a completely different manner of service than the performance of the commandments, he also warns against focusing on study to the exclusion of the performance of commandments. In fact, he states that one who studies yet does not perform commandments is considered as if he is a denier of the God of Israel.[119]

While among the Hasidic masters, emphasis upon action as the ultimate value was prevalent,[120] the idea that Torah study in and of itself is a religious experience whereby one can commune with the divine also developed. Unlike Rabbi Hayyim, whereby connection is via the understanding of the content of Torah, the Hasidic understanding of this form of worship by Torah study is as a medium of meditation upon the immanence of God and one's

[119] See Rabbi Norman Lamm's work, *Torah Lishma – Torah for Torah's Sake,* for further investigation on the thought of Rabbi Hayyim of Volozhin.

[120] See *Shulhan Arukh ha-Rav, Hilkhot Talmud Torah* by Rabbi Shneur Zalman, *Benei Yisaschar*, Tishrei 5:3 by Rabbi Tzvi Elimelech of Dinov, and *Beit ha-Levi* on Mishna *Avot* 2:2 by Rabbi Levi Yitzhak of Berdichev.

attachment to Him through the letters of the Torah. Rabbi Yaakov Yosef of Polennoye writes,

> [W]hen a man attaches himself to the form of the letters of the Torah, which is the bride, merging his total self with the inner essence of the Torah letters, this is the true spiritual coupling; that is shedding the garments of selfish motivation, benefit, or reward, and concentrating only on *lishma* – on the love of Torah and cleaving to her for her own sake. This is the root and purpose of everything.[121]

Within Hasidic writings, the study of Torah *lishma* became not necessarily a means for a person to receive instruction for future action; rather it became a means of revelation, both of God's presence and of man's innate love and fear of Him, and as a means to provoke divine communion within the act of study itself, thus diminishing the importance of study for the training of proper conduct in daily life.

Although among the followers of Rabbi Hayyim and the Hasidic masters, Torah study grew in significance at the expense of the importance of performance of the commandments, Rabbi Samson Raphael Hirsch, by defining Torah in terms of mental cognition, the root of Talmud (למד) in terms of habituation,[122] and the root of Education (חנך) in terms of practical training,[123] expanded the conception of Torah study to encompass not only the mental acquisition of Torah knowledge but also emphasize that the goal of study is the physical accustomization of a Torah way of life. Furthermore, in *The Nineteen Letters*, he put in the words of Naftali that despite the fact that the true speculation should lead to a more profound understanding of man's relationship to the world around him and his mission in life, sadly Torah study in his age was not directed towards such a goal. He states,

---

121 *Toledot Yaakov Yosef*, Shelah 4.
122 *The Pentateuch: Deuteronomy*, 41.
123 *Collected Writings* VII, 11.

> Judaism has no regard for the kind of speculation that does not aspire to contribute to active, productive life. It defines the limits of our understanding, and we are warned against misconceiving our intellectual powers and probing into bottomless depths, no matter what glittering constructions and theses such a quest may produce. Only an overcharged mind, subject to all the restraints imposed by man's nature but unaware of its own limitations, would feel the need for such speculation. To be sure, of late the Jewish way of thinking has predominantly been marked by abstruse musing; wide-awake observation of the world has been lacking. The goal of study has not been practical life, to understand the world and our duty in it; scholarship has become an end in itself, rather than a means toward an end, and only few have borne in mind its true objective.[124]

Through his teachings, Rabbi Samson Raphael Hirsch endeavored to return the focus of Torah study to its transformative capabilities in the life of a person through the training of his actions rather than through the act of study in and of itself.[125] His oft-quoted adage,

[124] *The Nineteen Letters*, 201.

[125] Interesting to note, where Maimonides writes that Talmud Torah invokes love of God and the performance of the commandments invokes fear of God, Rabbi Samson Raphael Hirsch argues that the opposite is the case. He writes, "But this fear of God, the Jewish fear of God, is not product of unclear vague feelings and moods or frame of mind; the fear of God has to be 'taught and learnt'...The fear of God is acquired by learning and practicing; the fear of God is a mental, a spiritual knowledge and a moral ability, as indeed both together comprise the full conception of [the root] *lamed-mem-dalet*. (*The Pentateuch: Deuteronomy*, 53)" Regarding love of God, he writes, "For the whole Torah is really in truth nothing but the revelation of how we have to prove our love for God, in our actions.... The *Ve-Ahavta Hashem b'khol lev* teaches us the *Torot*, the teachings which make our minds and hearts free from illusions and passions, fill them with truths and nobles thoughts; *Ahavta Hashem b'khol nefesh* teaches us the *Hukim*, the laws which limit and sanctify the development of our bodily physical being within the bounds of morality drawn by God, *Ahavta Hashem b'khol me'od* teaches us the *Mishpatim* and *Mitzvot*, the laws of justice and equity and commandments which build up our social life on the principles of justice and duty; and *Ahavta Hashem b'khol lev u-b'khol nefesh u-b'khol me'od* teaches us the *Edut*, the evidence of these truths and tasks represented by symbolic acts of recognition, and *Avodah*, our dedication to

"Good is Talmud Torah with Derekh Eretz," was meant to give credence to his belief that only through its manifestation in the world through practice did the study of Torah have a strong foundation.

Method versus Motive

Besides emphasizing man's intellect at the expense of intellect-directed action, Rabbi Soloveitchik assumes that possessing a certain intellectual perspective necessitates the focus of investigation – meaning that epistemological man can only involve himself in physical matters, while ontological man will ultimately search for a metaphysical answer to his ontological questions. While correlations between mathematical scientists who do not seek answers to theological questions and phenomenologists who have a theological bent exist, enough examples can show that correlation does not entail causation. Rather, it is the motive of the seeker, and not the method of analysis, that determines his search.

Rabbi Bahya ibn Paquda, after demonstrating that it is obligatory to reflect on creation – by which he means the study of the world in order to discover the ultimate purpose for which it was created – lists the various marks of wisdom in creation upon which one may reflect. The sixth "is the mark of wisdom manifest in the sciences, crafts, and industries with which the Creator, blessed be He, has equipped man to meet his needs, make a living, and gain other benefits, general and particular."[126] Through examining the world scientifically, Rabbi Bahya believes that one can develop an appreciation of the divine. Maimonides also advocates studying the physical sciences as preparation for the study of metaphysics; he writes, "Accordingly it is certainly necessary for whoever wishes to achieve human perfection to train himself at first in the art of logic,

---

all this by the procedures of the offerings which symbolize our seeking nearness to God by the service of our life and embrace the whole of our existence in every phase of it." (*The Pentateuch: Deuteronomy*, 97)

[126] *Duties of the Heart*, 185.

then in the mathematical sciences according to the proper order, then in the natural sciences, and after that in the divine science."[127] Where Rabbi Bahya sees scientific analysis as one of several ways to reach a theological appreciation, Maimonides views it as a requirement.

Even though he describes the dialectic as being as difficult today as it was during the times of Abraham and Moses,[128] perhaps Rabbi Soloveitchik's analysis is mainly directed towards the contemporary man of faith, who lives after what he calls a schism of enormous magnitude between the regional viewpoint of the empiricist and the universal vision of the metaphysician.[129] The difficulty in this assumption is that many modern scientists understand their work in terms of discovering God's laws of the universe, while many philosophers and theologians have abandoned the *mysterium tremendum*.

Henry Schaefer, Graham Perdue Professor of Chemistry and director of the Center for Computational Quantum Chemistry at the University of Georgia, describes his work as follows, "The significance and joy in my science comes in those occasional moments of discovering something new and saying to myself, 'So that's how God did it.' My goal is to understand a little corner of God's plan."[130] Where the halakhic man looks into the Torah to see the world, Schaefer looks into the world to discover God's natural law. Professor of Physics at Stanford University and 1981 Nobel Prize winner, Arthur Schawlow, states as a consequence of his work, "It seems to me that when confronted with the marvels of life and the universe, one must ask why and not just how. The only possible answers are religious.... I find a need for God in the universe and in my own life."[131] By his response, he could be considered an example of ontological man, though his methodology

---

[127] *Guide for the Perplexed*, 75.
[128] "Lonely Man of Faith," 2.
[129] *The Halakhic Mind*, 3.
[130] "The Creation," 56–64.
[131] *Cosmos, Bios, Theos*, 105.

defines him as the ideal epistemological man. For just one more example, Albert Einstein is quoted to have said regarding his work, alluding to Hillel, "I want to know how God created this world. I am not interested in this or that phenomenon, in the spectrum of this or that element. I want to know His thoughts. The rest are details."[132] According to Rabbi Soloveitchik's conception of epistemological man, a mathematical scientist could never have ventured out of his laboratory to imagine a God to which he could relate and in which he could discover himself. In the modern world, a scientist and a man of faith can be one and the same.

Although the modern ontological existentialist focuses on the question of human existence, in his perspective there is no purpose, indeed nothing at all, at its core. Existentialism seeks not the divine but a human way to counter the nothingness of being. Rather than escape the world as *homo religiosus*, the modern existentialist embraces the world. He recognizes that any search for meaning will result in a contradiction between his own desires and the reality of the world. Therefore, rather than sit in contemplation, the best he can make of his absurd situation is to live the aesthetic life of pleasure. As a modern existentialist, ontological man has justified epistemological man's way of life.

Radical theology is another example of ontological man rejecting the *mysterium tremendum* for a human-justified experience. Where *homo religiosus* searches for God outside physical experience, the radical theologian denies everything – especially God – that is outside the realm of his existential experience. Because God is wholly other and one cannot know His essence, the radical theologian feels justified in his claim that he cannot have a relationship with God. Only His absence is felt, and in His absence, man is completely autonomous in deciding the moral code for his life.

When experiencing the world for what it is, ontological man need not automatically take a step outside the physical realm to

---

[132] *The Expanded Quotable Einstein*, 202.

search for the supernatural. Similarly, epistemological man's analytical approach to understanding the world may very well prompt him to investigate He who created the laws which he has discovered. It is not the method of examination of the world that limits or allows metaphysical contemplation. Rather, it is the nature of the individual and the reason for his inquiry. The Kotzker Rebbe once asked his students, "Where is God?" Stunned, the students replied, "God is everywhere, of course!" The Rebbe replied, "No. God is only where you let Him in." Whichever method a man may use, if he wants to find God, he will, and if he wants to retreat from God, then God will withdraw in kind.

Individual versus Community

In order to define the proper approach for man towards others in his community, the Talmud[133] derives the idea that all Jews are responsible for one another from the verse, "With no one pursuing, they shall stumble over one another as before the sword."[134] In this case, one can only conclude that their collective downfall was their own doing, for if there is no one pursuing, what else could cause this to happen? It is explained in the *Midrash Tanhuma* that every Jew is responsible for every other; meaning that if there is one righteous person among the people, the rest will share in his merit. Similarly, if one person in the community sins, everyone will be punished if they were able to prevent him from doing so but did not.[135] An example of such an occurrence appears in the Book of Joshua. After the Israelites conquered the city of Jericho, Joshua proscribed all the spoils of the city and consecrated all the precious metals and metalwork to God. Achan son of Carmi, a descendant of Zerah of the tribe of Judah, took some of the proscribed items for himself. Because of his theft, the Israelites were not able to

---

133 BT *Shavuot* 39a

134 Leviticus 26:37.

135 *Midrash Tanhuma,* Nitzavim, Chapter 5.

conquer the relatively weak city of Ai and suffered casualties.[136] Everyone recognized that the defeat resulted from Achan's theft, and when the Reubenites, Gadites, and half of the tribe of Manasseh were later suspected of building an idolatrous altar, the other tribes used Achan's example to refute any claim as to why they need not involve themselves in the matter, saying:

> But do not rebel against Hashem, and do not rebel against us by building for yourselves an altar other than the altar of Hashem our Elohim. When Achan son of Zerah violated the proscription, anger struck the whole community of Israel. He was not the only one who perished for that sin.[137]

Rebellion against God is also a rebellion against the community because whether one rebels directly against the community or harms it indirectly through one's own sin, the entire community bears the consequences.

In order to prevent such disasters from occurring, God gives the Jews the following instruction: "Do not hate your kinsfolk in your heart. Reprove your kinsman and incur no guilt because of him. Do not take vengeance or bear a grudge against your countrymen. Love your fellow as yourself; I am Hashem your Elohim."[138] While it is an imperative to reprove one's fellow when he sins, the intent of the reproof is not self-serving. The Torah envelops the instruction to reprove with the commands not to hate the sinner, not to incur guilt because of him, not to bear a grudge, but rather to love him as oneself. Loving another as oneself is not imposing what one would like for oneself upon the other. Rather, it is recognizing a mutual commonality and thus appreciating the need to respect the other, or as Hillel described it, "What is hateful to you, do not do to your neighbor."[139] Reproof, therefore, is done with the interests of the reproved in mind; the seemingly selfish act

---

[136] Joshua 6–7.
[137] Joshua 22:19–20.
[138] Leviticus 19:17–18.
[139] BT *Shabbat* 31a.

of saving the community from harm becomes the altruistic act of caring for the religiously lapsed individual. One example is Moses, who challenged God by asking that his name be erased from the Torah during the sin of the Golden Calf. Another example is the Shunamite woman, who declined Elisha's offer of special recompense for all that she had done for him, saying, "I live among my people."[140]

The hero of "The Lonely Man of Faith" is the prophet Elisha. It is not because he was the founder of Judaism, nor the giver of the Torah, that he is made the ideal example. Rather, as Rabbi Soloveitchik describes him, he was an epistemological man who had recreated himself into the ideal.

> He was the son of a prosperous farmer, a man of property, whose interests were centered around this-worldly, material goods such as crops, livestock, and market prices. His objective was economic success, his aspiration – material wealth.[141]

When Elijah came to Elisha and "caste his mantle upon him," Elisha immediately recognized the value of his materialistic self-centeredness and, like the woman who went to Rabbi Hiyya in order to convert after experiencing true human relatedness,[142] abandoned his position of social status and gave his property away to the people. Elisha went even further than renouncing his materialistic attitude. He became an isolated individual.

> He bade farewell to father and mother and departed from their home for good. Like his master, he became homeless. Like his ancestor Jacob he became a 'straying Aramean' who took defeat and humiliation with charity and gratitude.[143]

---

140 II Kings 4:13.
141 "Lonely Man of Faith," 109–110.
142 BT *Menahot* 44a.
143 "Lonely Man of Faith," 111.

As ontological man, he could not communicate with his family or friends about who he was and what he was experiencing. Only Elijah could understand, for he too was a man of God. Teacher and disciple became a community unto themselves. Yet as a true halakhic man, Elisha returns to the community, although not to his previous position. He had left as a member of the community but returned as its adviser. Rabbi Soloveitchik concludes his essay with the following charge: "Is modern man of faith entitled to a more privileged position and a less sacrificial role?"[144] Halakhic man must also return to the epistemological community, ontologically lonely and socially alone, to teach and persuade those who will reject his words, simply because they cannot understand them.

The *leitmotif* of the Jewish leader retreating from society only to return to it with the mission of correcting its mores through example runs throughout Rabbi Soloveitchik's writings. The charismatic person, the unique personality who is able to restore the unity between the ethical and the esthetic thus returning the world to the ideal of creation,[145] must be transformed in the same manner as Elisha.

> The charismatic personality must disassociate himself from his national connections and completely free himself from the environment he was born and reared in. The chosen person severs his affiliation with his clan and friends; he deserts everybody in order to give himself up to his new friend, God. The first prerequisite for prophecy is loneliness.[146]

The reason for such separation is reflexive. For the charismatic man to completely relate to God, his dedication must be total. God does not allow any intrusion by society upon him.[147] Therefore, because

---

144 "Lonely Man of Faith," 112.
145 *The Emergence of Ethical Man,* 149.
146 *The Emergence of Ethical Man,* 150.
147 *The Emergence of Ethical Man,* 152.

God will not allow society to influence him, the charismatic man must refrain from influencing society during his transformation. As Rabbi Soloveitchik writes,

> The prophet must remove himself from his native environment. The environment into which we are born determines the way of our thinking, feeling, and striving. We think in terms of and via media with which we were confronted as a child...the person who finds God is homeless, fatherless, and childless – not biologically but spiritually. He is related neither to his parent nor to his child; he has to give up and disengage.[148]

Of the patriarch, Abraham, Rabbi Soloveitchik contends that he could not have received God's message if he had not retreated from society.[149] This idea is supported by the fact that the Torah records God's message that Abraham will become a great nation and his offspring will be as uncountable as the dust of the earth only after it records Terah's death and Lot's departure.

Physical separation, however, is not the essence of charismatic man's characterization.[150] Rather, it is a separation in outlook. He does not share the same frame of reference as others, yet he still shares a certain commonality with them. Rabbi Soloveitchik explains,

> The religious leader is a person who retreats from society into seclusion and loneliness. Again, this retreat is not

---

148 *Abraham's Journey*, 77–78.

149 *Abraham's Journey*, 84.

150 See *Abraham's Journey*, page 79, where he writes, "I must emphasize that the religious personality's disengagement from and renunciation of the finite experience does not entail a monastic philosophy of an ascetic way of life. Judaism, as is well known, has enjoined man to share with God in the works of creation, to involve himself fully in the cosmic occurrence. What I intend to convey by using the terms 'disengagement' and 'flight' is that man, in spite of his physical and mental participation in natural events and processes, must never deal in absolutes with regard to finite creation, must never ascribe unlimited worth and supremacy to human achievements, institutions and values."

> physical but axiological. Abraham dwelt in a new world of values that were alien to his society. He dealt with the same facts as his contemporaries, but interpreted these primordial facts differently – not so much in an intellectual or scientific sense, but in terms of their meaning and value.[151]

This commonality is key for his re-integration into society for the purposes of its improvement. Abraham did not live an ascetic life. He was wealthy, politically powerful, and socially influential. He lived among the other nations in Canaan, yet not with them. Through his deeds, he tried to create a community, whose membership would come from the very people whose company he had rejected and whose friendship and concern he had refused to acknowledge. In his new role, he "tried to rediscover them, to affiliate with them, to find a common language with them, to communicate his great message to them."[152]

Should the modern reader, confused by his own selfishness and searching for meaning in the narcissistic world in which he lives, be guided along the path towards Rabbi Soloveitchik's halakhic man? When a secular Jew has a moment of religious epiphany, should he leave his family, his support group, everything he has previously known, in order to transform himself under the auspices of a monastic religious institution? Even if we would agree that such is the correct path, are there enough caring and selfless teachers to give their disciples the same attention Elijah gave Elisha?

Furthermore, when the recreated halakhic man returns home from his yeshiva, he no longer can relate to his secular parents, as his essence is not communicable to those who are not part of his ontological community. He cannot simply choose not to interact with them – as much as this may be his preferred choice of action – since he is commanded to honor them and, as God's messenger, he

---

[151] *Abraham's Journey*, 80–81.
[152] *Abraham's Journey*, 86.

should want to assist them, along with everyone else, in perceiving the divinity within their own experience. With his new found religious responsibility and his lack of social communicability, his attitude towards his family and friends may become frustrating and even patronizing, and he may end up alienating himself and others by his own religious confidence.

One could argue that although the ideal of creating oneself as a halakhic man from modern secular origins will entail sacrifice, this is only because the background from which he begins is void of religious constitution. If, on the other hand, one were to live in a society where ontological man was not rejected and the duality of man were present, then, even in a community where not everyone had completely internalized the halakhic ideal to be considered a halakhic man, those few self-actualized people would not live in the same type of self-centered yet God-absorbed isolation as their modern counterpart. Rabbi Soloveitchik's writings do not seem to make such an argument. Rather, emphasis seems to be placed upon halakhic man's individuality, and the individual's own concern comes before that of the community.

In his explanation of the commandments to sacrifice the red heifer and the paschal lamb, Rabbi Soloveitchik asks whether it is the personal commitment to Torah or the national commitment to peoplehood that is greater for Jewish survival. One might initially think that the answer is obvious: both are equally important in order to maintain the Jewish people. Although intuitive, he would comfort himself in his quick response by remembering Rashi's commentary on the first verse of the Torah, in which he quotes a midrash which equates the Torah and Israel as the reason for the creation of the world. Commenting on the word "beginning," the midrash states, "[The world was created] for the sake of the Torah, which is called 'The beginning of His way,' and for the sake of Israel, who are called 'The beginning of His grain crop.'"[153] On the other hand, Rabbi Soloveitchik uses his explanation of the two

[153] *Genesis Rabbah* 1:6.

commandments to defend his claim that one's personal commitment to God and Torah precedes his affiliation to his people, and even the importance of his affiliation is vis-à-vis his personal commitment to God and Torah. He states, "The State and the community are important because, through the corporate group, the individual Jew is enabled to act heroically, not only on the collective, history-making level but also in his private life. Yet the relationship between the Jew and God is central. It precedes his relationship with his people, in which God is involved."[154] The emphasis on the individual, even when in the context of community, is of central importance to Rabbi Soloveitchik's conception of the religious man. Elsewhere, Rabbi Soloveitchik writes,

> Moreover, the Halakhah is concerned with man as centered mainly on the individual. Man is neither an idea, like humanity, whose praise Plato and the Greek philosophers sang, nor a supra-individual (*sic*) unity, like society, a community, which many philosophical systems, including that of Marx, have idealized and idolized. They sang the praise of society, which is supra-individual unity. The Halakhah insists that nothing, not the idea nor the collective, should supplant the single, transient, fleeting, frail, individual 'who is here today and tomorrow is in the grave,' who today is here on the platform and the next day, who knows where he will end up. He occupies a dominant position in the Halakhah, and his role is central and indispensable. Of course, the Halakhah has not overlooked the community, particularly the community of the committed and the elected, as the bearer to the Divine eternal message. Yet, the individual constitutes a reality,

[154] *Reflections of the Rav*, 113.

> whose ontic legitimacy must not be questioned, and whose interest the Halakhah, like a devoted mother, has at heart.[155]

Although individuality may protect the community from blind social conformity, taken to the extreme it can manifest itself in individualism at the expense of communal involvement, as seen in the following examples.

Because his own study of Torah is so important, halakhic man does not serve in a rabbinical capacity. Unlike Moses, who sat from morning until evening settling disputes among the people, halakhic man sits by himself or with several others who are reluctant to make practical decisions. If necessity, as Rabbi Soloveitchik puts it, "compels them to disregard their preference and to render practical decisions, this is only a small, insignificant responsibility which does not stand at the center of their concerns."[156] To avoid serving in a judicial capacity because the responsibility is small and insignificant seems to contradict what the Torah teaches about the importance and great responsibility of a judge. Rabbi Jacob ben Asher, in the beginning of his work *Hoshen Mishpat*, interprets the Mishna in *Avot* that states, "Rabban Shimon ben Gamliel says: On three things the world endures: judgment, truth, and peace,"[157] as follows:

> That due to the judges judging between men the world endures… and this is the intention of our Sages, of blessed memory, when they said: Any judge who judges according to absolute truth is as if he were made a partner with the Holy One, blessed be He, in the creation of the world.

While it is true that Halakha stipulates that it was the habit of sages of previous generations to avoid judicial appointments, it was not because they saw such positions as small and insignificant. On the contrary, due to their own humility they felt that they were not

---

155 *Out of the Whirlwind*, 94–95. Also from the typescript of an unpublished lecture, "Mental Health and Halakha," delivered in December 1961. Found in "On the Jewish People in the Writings of Rabbi Joseph B. Soloveitchik," 41, n. 3.
156 *Halakhic Man*, 24.
157 Mishna *Avot* 1:18.

worthy of such a great responsibility. To see the context of why the rabbis would flee from judging, one must see both the particular Halakha on the matter and the one preceding it, as written by Rabbi Joseph Karo.

> When judges judge, they must sit in fear and awe, each wrapped in his *tallit*, in a serious state of mind. The judge is forbidden to let himself forget the gravity of the task at hand. Neither is he allowed to sit in court and speak of matters that are lacking in substance. A judge should imagine that a sword is resting on his throat and that purgatory is open before him under his feet. He needs to know who he is about to judge, and before Whom, and to Whom he will have to give an accounting in the future if he deviates from the exact line of justice. Any judge who does not judge truthfully to law cause the Divine Presence to remove itself from the Jewish people. If a judge unjustly takes money from one litigant and gives it to the other litigant, the Holy One, blessed be He, takes his soul from him. Any judge who judges litigation truthfully, even if it is only once, it is as if he brought rectification to the entire world. He causes the Divine Presence to rest upon the Jewish people. It was the way of the sages of old to flee from being appointed as judges. They would trouble themselves to not sit on any court until they were certain that there was no one as qualified as they and that if they refrained from sitting on the court, justice would be perverted. Even so, they would not accept the task of being a judge until the people pressured them and exhorted them.[158]

The sages did not need to be pressured because they thought the position beneath them. They held the position in such high regard that they did not believe themselves capable for such a role. The idea that helping others resolve their disputes is less important than

[158] *Shulhan Arukh, Hoshen Mishpat*, 8:2–3.

one's own religious journey contradicts the examples of all the Jewish leaders in history who served in a judicial capacity[159] and denigrates the value of community for the sake of the individual.

Halakhic man's lack of concern for others is not limited to the wider community; it affects even his family. The intensity of his personal devotion to God is starkly illustrated by the following emotionally wrenching example Rabbi Soloveitchik gives of the strength of character halakhic man possesses even at a time of great personal anguish. I quote it at length in order that it will impress fully upon the reader.

> The beloved daughter of R. Elijah Pruzna [Feinstein] took sick about a month before she was to be married, and after a few days was rapidly sinking. R. Elijah's son entered into the room where R. Elijah, wrapped in *tallit* and *tefillin*, was praying with the congregation, to tell him that his daughter was in her death throes. R. Elijah went into his daughter's room and asked the doctor how much longer it would be until the end. When he received the doctor's reply, R. Elijah returned to his room, removed his Rashi's *tefillin*, and quickly put on the *tefillin* prescribed by Rabbenu Tam, for immediately upon his daughter's death he would be an *onen*, a mourner whose dead relative has not yet been buried, and as such would be subject to the law that an *onen* is exempt from all the commandments. After he removed his second pair of *tefillin*, wrapped them up, and put them away, he entered his dying daughter's room, in order to be present at the moment when his most beloved daughter of all returned her soul to its Maker. We have here great strength and presence of mind, the acceptance of the divine decree with love, the consciousness of the law and the judgment, the might and power of the Halakha, and faith, strong like flint.[160]

---

[159] See beginning of Rabbi Jacob ben Asher's *Hoshen Mishpat.*

[160] *Halakhic Man*, 77–78.

How strong was the character of halakhic man! Knowing that his daughter was about to die, he would not abandon his attachment to God. On the contrary, he bound himself to God through the *tefillin* prescribed by Rabbenu Tam, and only afterwards would he seek solace in attending to his most beloved daughter. Even as he left his personal communion with God, he did not hasten. He wrapped his *tefillin* carefully and put them away, showing them proper respect.

To fully understand the meaning of this story, one must first understand its halakhic background. It is written in the *Shulhan Arukh* that there is a religious obligation to visit the sick and that whoever increases his visitation is considered praiseworthy.[161] Visiting the sick is considered comparable to concentration in prayer in that one enjoys only the fruits of its reward in this world, while one receives the principal reward in the World to Come.[162] In the Talmud, visiting the sick is considered as one of the ways in which one can imitate the attributes of God.[163] Rabbi Akiva is quoted as saying that one who does not visit the sick is like a shedder of blood, and Rabbi Dimi is quoted as saying that he who visits the sick causes him to live, while he who does not causes him to die.[164] Whether the imperative of visiting the sick is of Torah or rabbinic origin is a debate among the Rishonim. However, even those who argue that it is of rabbinic origin agree that it is a rabbinic manifestation of the Torah law to love one's neighbor like oneself.[165] As soon as death is perceived to be near, Halakha instructs that people should not separate themselves from the sick person, so that his soul does not depart while he is alone.[166]

---

161 *Shulhan Arukh*, *Yoreh Deah* 335:1–2.
162 BT *Shabbat* 127a.
163 BT *Sotah* 14a.
164 BT *Nedarim* 40a.
165 Maimonides, *Book of Commandments,* Root Two.
166 *Shulhan Arukh*, *Yoreh Deah* 339:4.

The dispute between Rashi and Rabbenu Tam regarding the order of the paragraphs in the *tefillin* stems from a disagreement interpreting the following passage in the Talmud.

> Our Rabbis taught: What is the order [of the four Scriptural portions in the head-tefillah]? 'Sanctify unto Me' and 'And it shall be when the Lord shall bring thee' are on the right, while 'Hear' and 'And it shall come to pass if ye shall hearken diligently' are on the left. But there has been taught just the reverse? – Abaye said: This is no contradiction, for in the one case the reference is to the right of the reader, whereas in the other it is to the right of the one that wears them; the reader thus reads them according to their order.[167]

Rashi interprets the expression, "the reader thus reads them according to their order," that the sections in the *tefillin* should be written in the order that they are found in the Torah, and the one not wearing the *tefillin* would read the passages from right to left. On the other hand Rabbenu Tam, taking issue with description of having two passages on the right and two on the left, prescribes that the order should be from the outside inward, so that "Sanctify unto Me" is to the extreme right, "And it shall be when the Lord shall bring thee" in the inside right, "Hear" is to the extreme left, and "And it shall come to pass if ye shall hearken diligently" to the interior left. Like Rashi, Rabbenu Tam interprets the final statement to confirm that the correct order, albeit as he prescribes it, is from the perspective of the one who is not wearing the *tefillin*.

Although the ruling of the *Shulhan Arukh* is according to Rashi's interpretation, those who fear Heaven and are steadfast and reputed in their piety are recommended to wear both the *tefillin* of Rashi and Rabbenu Tam.[168] The reason for wearing both is not because both

---

[167] BT *Menahot* 34b.

[168] See *Shulhan Arukh*, *Orah Hayyim*, Chapter 34, and *Shulhan Arukh ha-Rav*, *Orah Hayyim*, Chapter 34.

are required according to Halakha. One makes a blessing only on Rashi's *tefillin* and Rabbenu Tam's *tefillin* is put on only after prayers.[169] It is universally accepted that, according to Halakha, only Rashi's *tefillin* need be worn. The reason that it is considered a good practice to wear his *tefillin* even though Halakha does not rule in favor of it is because Rabbenu Tam's *tefillin* was worn in many communities before the disagreement was resolved.[170]

From the halakhic background of this incident, the priorities of halakhic man become clear. He would rather bind himself to God through his *tefillin* prescribed by Rabbenu Tam, which is neither a fulfillment of a commandment nor even a rabbinic enactment, than give comfort to his own daughter, which at the very least is still a rabbinic manifestation of a Torah command. Halakhic man does not have the courage to surrender his personal desires in order to fulfill the commandments. He has the fortitude to choose the commandments that are between man and God over those that are between man and man.

The ability for halakhic man to emphasize his own personal religious experience over one based in communal action, even when that community is the family, is based upon his view of his relationship to others and to God. As seen above regarding the epistemological man's community and the ontological man's community, the general construct of community is utilitarian. Man, regardless of which typology is referred, desires to be part of a community solely because he is unable to survive alone. For epistemological man, survival is of a physical nature, and for ontological man, it is in terms of existential self-definition. Building

---

[169] It is possible to wear both pairs of tefillin simultaneously. However, when they are worn together, preference is giving to Rashi's tefillin.

[170] *Igrot Moshe, Orah Hayyim,* 4:9. While Rabbi Moshe Feinstein calls wearing Rabbenu Tam's *tefillin* only a stringent custom, the *Mishna Berurah* implies that one should have in mind when wearing Rabbenu Tam's *tefillin* that he is doing so because of a doubt in the law. However, his intention is not to doubt the veracity of ruling in favor of Rashi's *tefillin.* Rather, it is to avoid other legal difficulties due to wearing Rabbenu Tam's *tefillin,* despite the fact that Halakha rules in favor of Rashi. See *Biur Halakha, Orah Hayyim,* Chapter 34.

a community based upon true consideration and love for another is, Rabbi Soloveitchik admits, extremely difficult. He writes,

> [T]he natural love of the members of one's group is simply a feeling of solidarity that emerges from a shared sense of history and fate. In truth, this love is really, in its uniqueness, self-love. The act of projection brings the I who is loved by himself, to the other, for he sees a mirror of himself in the other. This egotistical connection does not obligate the person in actions towards the other individual…However, the command 'Love thy neighbor as thyself' (in all its meanings, whether as per Hillel the elder in its negative sense, or in its positive meanings as formulated in the *Rambam's* Code, *Hilkot Avel*, Chapter 14) demands of the individual a non-egotistical love toward the other, and obligates the individual to perform concrete actions. According to *Rambam* (in *Hilkot Avel*) the love for the other is the basis for all of society. Therefore the love of one's fellow Jew is achieved only through sacrifice and hard work. It is an extremely exalted level of morality…[171]

No matter what emphasis one puts upon the greater community, if the general – since the true ideal love of another is so hard to attain – perspective is to see others through an egotistical connection, then fulfillment of religious obligations will always prioritize those with individual satisfaction over those of individual sacrifice for communal betterment. It is true that Rabbi Soloveitchik states that the "best virtues which are at the apex of our ethical hierarchy – compassion, love, sharing in another's travail and distress – are derived from *middat ha-hesed*, the attribute of kindness; they would lose their significance should the individual live in isolation."[172] To perform acts of *hesed* is to imitate the divine, yet one cannot relegate inter-personal acts to the realm of *hesed*, able to be attained by only

---

[171] *Community, Covenant and Commitment*, 334.
[172] *Days of Deliverance*, 114–115.

those who have reached the pinnacle of self-perfection, and ignore them in the realm of Halakha.

Even in the realm of the marriage community, where one would think that because husband and wife share a life together and become "one flesh," or at least in the parent-child relationship, where each sees himself as an extension of the other, there would be some sort of existential unification that would produce an absolute bond creating an example to extend to the broader family of the Jewish community. Although Rabbi Soloveitchik calls a marriage a covenantal community,[173] and part of the great *masorah* community that passes the covenant from generation to generation,[174] the individual, and his relationship with God, still precludes full integration into a family. He writes,

> Marriage, notwithstanding its covenantal character, is not an institution of absolute worth. There is an objective bond, yet it is confined to kerygmatic Eve and Adam who can standardize and objectify their experiences. It does not reach into the very core of the personality, which remains a *mysterium*, a subjective experience inexpressible and outside of all media of externalization and objectification. Only social Adam and Eve are wedded; lonely Adam and Eve have never joined this community. Therefore, marriage is changeable because it does not embrace the whole of man.[175]

Even to one's own child, to whom he passes on the *masorah* and instructs in order to achieve religious self-perfection in the future, one cannot give his complete self. To Reverend James S. Walsh, in his explanation of the significance and the lesson of the commandment to redeem the first-born son, Rabbi Soloveitchik writes,

---

173 *Family Redeemed*, 47.
174 *Family Redeemed*, 29–30.
175 *Family Redeemed*, 62–63.

> When the husband and father who is passionately in love with his wife and children, enjoying the community awareness of the family, the serenity of a home life, the sense of irrevocable commitment and devotion that hovers over his intimate circle, realizes that perfect fellowship between and of finite individual beings is an impossibility and that only in God can he find absolute friendship and understanding, a great offering is brought on the altar of the Creator. If he understands that notwithstanding the emotional closeness, the warmth of the sentiment and deep involvement with each other, he, and for that reason, each one of his household, must still lead a solitary existence for him or herself because all human emotional bonds are relative, that only God will never forsake him, 'When my mother and father forsake my, then the Lord will take me up,' he acts sacrificially.[176]

No matter whether he sees himself in relation to his family, his community, or the world, man must see himself as alone and lonely in order to remain fixated on the One God who desires him wholly and without intrusion.

Rabbi Soloveitchik defines the halakhic man in terms of his individuality and his focus upon his own religious experience. Understanding the notion that to connect with God one must be free of other connections, he knows that only he is responsible for his own destiny. Because his words are so poignant, I will quote him directly.

> But there is another man, one who does not require the assistance of others, who does not need the support of the species to legitimate his existence. Such a man is no longer a prisoner of time but is his own master. He exists not by virtue of the species, but solely on account of his own individual worth. His life is replete with creation and renewal, cognition and profound understanding. He lives not on account of his having been born but for the sake of

---

[176] *Community, Covenant and Commitment*, 299–300.

> life itself and so that he may merit thereby the life in the world to come. He recognizes the destiny that is his, his obligation and task in life. He understands full well the dualism running through his being and that choice which has been entrusted to him.... He does not simply abandon himself to the rule of the species but blazes his own individual trail.... This is the man of God.[177]

In becoming the man of God, I fear that I cannot see how he has remained a man of the people as well. If all Jews are responsible for each other, how can he blaze his own individual trail? Surely, the halakhic man knows that "he who does not fulfill the commandments together with them, does not take part in their hardships, or join in their [communal] fasts, but rather goes on his own individual path... does not have a portion in the world to come."[178] When Ruth told Naomi, "your people will be my people and your God will be my God," she merited having King David and the Messiah as her descendants. If she had only said "your God will be my God," could we have expected the same result?[179]

---

177 *Halakhic Man*, 127–128.

178 *Hilkhot Teshuva* 3:11.

179 In "*Kol Dodi Dofek*," Rabbi Soloveitchik discusses the shared experience of the Jewish community and Job's suffering because of his individualism. However, shared experience is emphasized within the framework of what he calls a community of fate and not a congregation of destiny. For Rabbi Soloveitchik, a community of fate is a defensive community, and, in the individual sphere, man must remove himself from fate to live in the ethico-halakhic rubric of destiny. While in the congregation of destiny there is an experience of unity based upon the community's betrothal to God, nevertheless, separation within the congregation is what makes each member great and sanctified within the solitude of his own consciousness. In his mention of the solitude of Moses, Elijah, and Abraham to underscore the greatness of the individual within the congregation of destiny, he gives further support to the idea that the Jewish leader, while a congregant, is very much alone in his religious development.

RABBI BERKOVITS AND THE AUTHENTIC JEW

RABBI BERKOVITS shares Rabbi Soloveitchik's opinion that modern society has usurped the realm in which sincere religion could be expressed, leaving in its wake either relative utilitarianism devoid of moral values or a religion of convenience rather than commitment.[1] In dealing with the current condition, however, Rabbi Berkovits differs from Rabbi Soloveitchik in that he neither admits of a dialectical vacillating between interaction and withdrawal nor promotes confining oneself to a displaced position of moral authority. In order to survive both the spiritual and physical crisis of the modern era, he contends that Jews must examine their tradition in light of the world around them in order to apply the values of Judaism properly to the world in which they live. Only then can they become authentic Jews.

Before the modern Jew is able to regain his authenticity, he must first understand what it is to be a Jew vis-à-vis Judaism, the Jewish people, and the land of Israel. Rabbi Berkovits emphasizes that one cannot separate the Judaic triad without perverting the essence of what each represents. Judaism, as we will see in discussing his conception of Halakha, is a religion that incorporates the entirety of man in fulfillment of its commandments, which are both socially directed and aim for the progression of man's moral

[1] For Rabbi Soloveitchik's view, see "Lonely Man of Faith," 103. For Rabbi Berkovits's view of the modern era's moral collapse see *Crisis and Faith*. For his view of contemporary religious expression as being one of convenience and not commitment, see "From the Temple to Synagogue and Back" and "Jewish Education in a World Adrift."

development throughout history. As the observant Jew adheres to a religion of purposeful action rather than of dogmatic creed, he must surround himself with others who share the same divinely-inspired moral responsibility to be able to influence history as Judaism dictates. Communal structure becomes essential. While many have proposed that one man can change the world, history testifies that this will happen only when many others join him in his cause. Rabbi Berkovits remarks, "For the deed to be effective, it must not remain the act of an individual, but must become that of a community. The deed makes history if it is the materialization of the desire and will of a community of people joined together in a common cause."[2] The Jewish religion emphasizes the social and community-oriented character of its practice not only through commandments relating to interpersonal matters; even ritual commandments such as prayer, which could be considered the most personal and individualistic of all acts between man and God, requires public interaction, for the ideal performance of the commandment is when one prays with a quorum.

The absolute necessity of a Jewish people, rather than a congregation of individuals who practice Judaism, is demonstrated by the fact that Judaism was founded not by a religious leader who assembled disciples, but rather by a patriarch. What better place to find a group of individuals who share a common goal and mutual interests than in a family? It is true that Abraham and Sarah attracted converts during their stay in Haran and that a significant minority left Egypt together with the tribes of Israel, but normative Jewish practice never minimized the emphasis on the family in favor of a covenantal community. Rather, converts to Judaism become as much a part of the Jewish people as Abraham's direct descendants.[3]

Judaism's exotericism and familial predilection necessitates encompassing the entirety of experience. Ritual and sacrament

---

[2] *God, Man and History*, 138.

[3] For further analysis of this idea, see Maimonides's "Letter to Obadiah."

alone cannot instill all the social norms for proper communal living. Not only must there be laws of daily conduct, but society requires laws determining marriage and family life, torts, business, and judicial procedure, not to mention many other areas of public jurisdiction. Jewish thought must also be developed by the community in order to reinforce Jewish ideals and to give spirit to the letter of the legal code. Furthermore, and arguably most importantly for Rabbi Berkovits, laws and religious texts must not only be studied for theological edification; they must be lived to achieve their purpose. To do so, however, requires that the Jewish community have control over the territory in which it resides.

> Only the group that wields a measure of control over its own destiny sufficient to enable it to order the varied manifestations of its life in accordance with such an all-encompassing faith is in a position to realize Judaism as a whole. To the extent to which such control and authority are lacking, Judaism remains unrealizable. But realization is essential to Judaism and the group that may most completely achieve it is a people sovereign in its own home.[4]

It is obvious that the societal laws of Judaism cannot be fulfilled in an ideal manner when the Jewish people do not control their surroundings. However, in such an environment even laws of personal daily conduct are perverted to meet the demands of the dominant society. Rabbi Berkovits gives as an example the observance of the Sabbath.[5] While many Sabbath observant Jewish communities in the Diaspora exist, because individuals in those communities work in a greater society that does not rest on Saturday, the Sabbath becomes subject to accommodation rather than honor. To understand its subordinate position, one need not go further than the Broadway-Seventh Avenue Line in Manhattan

---

[4] "The Galut of Judaism," 226–227.
[5] *God, Man and History,* 139; "The Galut of Judaism," 227.

or the Far Rockaway Branch of the Long Island Railroad on a Friday afternoon to see the horde of Sabbath-observant businessmen racing home before the eighteen minutes after candle-lighting have ended. Only in a society that dictates its own holidays and whose economy yields to the demands of the Sabbath does Rabbi Berkovits foresee the possibility of Sabbath observance as Judaism has meant for it. Similarly, in order for the entirety of Jewish law and thought to be alive, the Jewish people must live in a sovereign Jewish country.

Although Judaism demands that Jews live in a sovereign Jewish land ruled by Jewish law, contrary to both ecclesiasm and nationalism, it produces neither a theocracy nor a secular nation reinforced by civil religion, but what Rabbi Berkovits calls a God-centered republic. Using the biblical declaration that the Jews shall be a kingdom of priests and a holy nation to justify his claim, he writes, "This kingdom of priests is not a society in which a priestly caste rules over a lay population in the name of some god. A holy nation is a realm in which all are priests. But where all are priests, all are servants – and God alone rules."[6] As a holy nation, the Jewish people look not to its own survival and self-interest. Instead, in serving the will of its leader, its concern is for all of God's creation, and thus it serves as a means to achieve God's purpose in history. To accomplish its international effect, the Jewish people must live with the rest of humankind, for just as Jewish individuals must unite to be able to fulfill Judaism's requirements properly, so must the Jewish people live among the nations in order to fulfill Judaism's purpose. As a nation, it must set an example to the others, showing the world how to live in a God-centered society.

Rabbi Berkovits's description of the holy nation's role in history lends itself to the paradoxical relationship between Jewish universalism and chosenness. Rather than perceiving the paradox as a coexistence of two mutually exclusive concepts, Rabbi Berkovits

---

[6] *God, Man and History*, 140–141.

explains the relationship as being one of presupposition. The idea that Jews are the chosen people has no theological or metaphysical import; it explains nothing about God or the nature of the universe.[7] For history to progress towards a universal God-oriented society, a nation must be chosen to teach the world how such a society would look. Chosenness does not imply spiritual superiority. Rather, it connotes responsibility.

> Since, however, the 'God of the Spirit of all Flesh' was associated with justice and righteousness, mercy and loving-kindness, the election of Israel could not have meant the abandonment by the Almighty of the rest of the world. The just and gracious God cannot give up His responsibility toward any part of His creation. Therefore, the essence of the idea of a Chosen People derives from the notion that the Father of all mankind single out one of His children for some reason or purpose.[8]

Rabbi Berkovits interprets the concept of "holy nation" in the same manner. By defining the word "holy" as that which has been removed from its original context and placed in a context that God has designated,[9] Rabbi Berkovits removes any sense of inherency. That holiness is derived and not innate is demonstrated by the frequent association between the command that Israel be holy and the command to listen to God's voice and do His will.[10] Spiritual closeness to God is, by this definition, a consequence of holiness and not a prerequisite. As both the concept of a "holy nation" and the "chosen people" do not communicate anything about the essence of the Jewish people, Rabbi Berkovits contends,

> It is, however, not altogether irrelevant to consider that Israel was not really 'chosen,' but rather came into being by having been chosen. God never chose the Jews; rather, any

[7] *Judaism – Fossil or Ferment?*, 65.
[8] *Judaism – Fossil or Ferment?*, 65.
[9] *Man and God*, 179.
[10] *Man and God*, 185.

people whom God chose was to become the Jewish people.[11]

As to why the ultimate choice was the family of Abraham, Rabbi Berkovits dares not make any assumptions, nor does it seem to matter. What is significant is only that it was chosen and the responsibility that being chosen entails.

Because the universal outlook of the Jewish people contradicts the nationalistic perspective of the rest of the world, until the time when the world reaches the goal of history, the Jewish people are destined to be persecuted by the other nations. Unwilling to succumb to cultural pressures by the surrounding nations at the expense of its own mission, other nations perceive Jewish intractability as jingoism rather than as ecumenism. Regarding this "clash of civilizations," Rabbi Berkovits writes, "The conflict, at times, is unavoidable, and can have tragic consequences for the 'one people.' In the history of Israel, these consequences are responsible for the exile; they have created the wandering Jew."[12] In fact, Rabbi Berkovits argues, exile is an essential component in the historical development of mankind. While Jews do say in their prayers that exile is a consequence of their sins, their admission must be seen in the context of "rigorous self-criticism" when facing God in prayer. From the moment God foretold to Abraham of the exilic inception of the Jewish people, exile was destined to play an essential part in their role in history.

Exile cannot be a permanent phenomenon; when the goal of history is realized, the Jewish people will once again live together in the ideal environment of a sovereign Jewish land under Jewish law. "From the very beginning, Judaism contained within itself the likelihood of Exile as well as the certainty of Redemption and to be a Jew meant to accept the one and to wait for the other."[13] In order to allay the tension between the necessity of a sovereign Jewish

---

[11] *God, Man and History*, 144.
[12] *God, Man and History*, 145.
[13] "The Galut of Judaism," 228.

state both so that Judaism can be practiced properly and for it to fulfill its historic purpose in the international arena, and the teleological necessity of exile, Rabbi Berkovits must differentiate between an ideal Judaism, practiced by ideal Jews in their ideal Jewish land, and authentic Judaism, practiced by authentic Jews in exile. It is important to note the contradiction created by the necessity of sovereignty to fulfill the purpose of Judaism and exile as a historical inevitability. Rabbi Berkovits responds with the argument that the inability of the Jewish people to affect history as a collective does not absolve any individual Jew of his own historical responsibility. Each one must do whatever he can to achieve the recognition of God in the world, regardless of the extent to which his actions are effective

> The goal of human history may never be achieved, the unity of mankind may never become a complete reality, and the day on which 'the Eternal shall be King over all the earth' may yet require a culminating act of divine grace and love; but man's own responsibility never ceases, for his opportunity to bring the goal closer to realization is never lost.... Universal reconciliation may never be achieved by man alone, yet it is always *achievable* by him.[14]

The acknowledgement that he is responsible to affect universal recognition and to practice Judaism in a manner that allows for the realization of its purpose, though modified by circumstances, defines the authentic Jew throughout the various stages of history.

Jewish law by itself does not make Judaism authentic simply because life does not consist of regulated action alone. In order for one to be an authentic Jew, the manner in which his thoughts are formulated, communicated, and implemented must reflect a Jewish perspective, yet they must also be intelligible given the society in which he resides. Consequently, authentic Judaism does not exist in the absolute. There are as many authentic Judaisms as there are societies in which authentic Jews live.

---

[14] *God, Man and History*, 156–157.

> Ever since Sinai we have witnessed an entire series of Jewries, all based on Torah and Halakha, yet differing from each other in outlook, attitude, and their understanding of Judaism. Babylonian Jewry was not Spanish Jewry; and the Spanish Jewry of Gabirol, the Ibn Ezras, of Hisdai Ibn Shaprut, Halevi and Maimonides, was not the Central European Jewry of the authors of the *Tosafot.* Nearer to our own times, the halakhic Jewries of Eastern Europe were not the halakhic Jewries of a Samson Raphael Hirsch or an Ezriel Hildesheimer. There were vast differences between them in the understanding of Halakha, in the philosophical interpretation of the teachings and faith of Judaism; considerable divergences in their respective attitudes toward the outside world, far-reaching ideological disagreements concerning secular studies and professional pursuits.[15]

In short, Rabbi Berkovits calls authentic Judaism the application of Torah to the "market places" of existence, meaning the everyday life of the contemporary situation. Authentic Judaism encounters the present; it does not ignore it in favor of an illusory and inapplicable past.

Nowhere is the encounter with the residing society more evident than in the history of Jewish thought. From Rabbi Saadia Gaon's use of Kalam to Maimonides's embrace of Aristotelian principles, from Rabbi Solomon ibn Gabirol's Neo-Platonism to Rabbi Samson Raphael Hirsch's Kantian perspective, each Jewish thinker attempted to portray Judaism through the philosophical language that was in fashion at the time. What allows for differing expressions of Judaism to claim authenticity is recognition in the absolute Jewish concepts of God, Israel, and Torah. In allowing for freedom of expression in the realm of interpretation and not of content, Rabbi Berkovits contends, "Any interpretation, from whatever foreign source it may originate, that acknowledges God, Israel, and the Torah as historic realities and attempts to provide

[15] "Authentic Judaism and Halakha," 66.

metaphysical or theological corollary to the facts and events for which they stand, may well be incorporated in a Jewish philosophy."[16] Halakhic directive also changes given historical and geographical conditions, as will be shown in discussing Rabbi Berkovits's conception of Halakha, yet not with the same salience of foreign influence. Judaism can imbibe externalities yet remain authentic simply because it must be able to be practiced authentically in exile. If it could not realize its purpose during the requisite exile because of its inability to encounter foreign culture, the Jewish people would fail in their role to achieve God's goal for history.

> A negative attitude to secular knowledge will not only prevent the peoples' seeing in Judaism 'our wisdom and our understanding,' it will not even allow the Jewish people to gain a comprehensive Jewish world-view. It may lose us the historic Israel and replace it by a handful of life-estranged Jewish sectarians.[17]

If they wish to have an influence on life both as a nation and in exile, Jews must live in and must engage the world. They "must speak in the language of man" in order to create either a model civilized Jewish society or to influence the societies in which they live.

Engagement with the world, however, has a correlative condition. The more oppressive the external force, the farther inward the Jew must turn in order to maintain his authenticity. In the extreme situation in which a Jew is about to be murdered on account of his Jewishness, the authentic Jew will ignore all externalities, his practice of Judaism becoming a *kiddush Hashem*, a sanctification of God's name. Rabbi Berkovits tells of the martyrdom of Rabbi Akiva to illustrate this concept. The Talmud states that the time to recite the *Shema* arrived when the Romans took Rabbi Akiva to his execution, and so, at this moment, Rabbi

---

16 "What is Jewish Philosophy?," 121.
17 "An Integrated Jewish World View," 15.

Akiva recited the *Shema*. His recital was not the dramatic declaration of God's unity that one would imagine from a defiant zealot. He said the *Shema* as he had said it the day before and the day before that. On this most extraordinary of days, he kept to his daily routine. By ignoring his situation instead of responding to it, he demonstrated that the universal purpose of Judaism remains constant no matter what external incongruity poses a threat. God must be recognized at all times. This is the true sanctification of God's name.

> Continuing with the 'routine' of Jewish existence and ignoring the world that is bent on crushing the Jew is one of the marks of *kiddush Hashem*.... Sanctification of God's name in this sense is not one final heroic act of affirmation. It may be a form of behavior and daily conduct.[18]

The importance of engaging the world is to teach the nations to acknowledge God; when that message falls on deaf ears, there is no point in continuing to communicate.

Rabbi Berkovits's conception of the authentic Jew attempts to exchange sentimentalism for a focus on present circumstances, justifying the reconstruction of traditional Judaism to meet the challenges of contemporary society in order for Judaism to remain relevant and meaningful in the new environment of modernity. His decision of focus, however, deemphasizes responsibility for why Jews are the chosen people and for the exile, as well as influences the perspective Rabbi Berkovits's authentic Jew would have on the significance of the land of Israel.

The Jewish People

While it is true that the Jews could not become the chosen people without God's having chosen them explicitly, in broaching yet not affirming that God chose them because they were the most qualified choice,[19] Rabbi Berkovits suppresses any warrant for the

---

[18] *Essential Essays*, 330.

[19] *God, Man and History*, 144.

divine choice of the Jews to be the chosen people. The Torah twice mentions that God had chosen the Jews to be His holy nation,[20] but only once gives His reasons.

> It is not because you are the most numerous of peoples that Hashem set His heart on you, and chose you, indeed you are the smallest of peoples; but it was because Hashem loved you and because He kept the oath which He swore to your fathers that Hashem freed you with a mighty hand and redeemed you out of the house of bondage, from the hand of Pharaoh king of Egypt.[21]

Contrary to Rabbi Berkovits's claim that the Jewish people came into being by having been chosen, the Torah specifically gives two reasons for God's decision to choose the already-existing Jewish people: God loved them and God had obligated Himself to choose them via the covenant that He had made with Abraham, Isaac and Jacob. Either reason would have sufficed for the Jewish people to be chosen; if God loved them, no covenant was necessary, and if God chose the Jews in order to uphold the covenant, love is irrelevant. The fact that the Torah gives as a reason both God's love and His covenant demonstrates the worthiness of the Jewish people in their own right, and not only as descendants of their forefathers, to be chosen to perform God's will on earth.

To explain why Abraham was more fit than any other to be the progenitor of the chosen nation, tradition accounts that Abraham, rather than God, initiated the historical relationship. God addressed Abraham only after he had already acknowledged His existence by his own discovery and had begun to publicly challenge the rampant idolatry of his day.[22] His public persona, whether it be through proselytizing or through protecting others despite their immorality, differentiated him from all other righteous prophets before him

---

[20] Deuteronomy 7:6, 14:2.

[21] Deuteronomy 7:7–8

[22] *Hilkhot Avodat Kokhavim* 1:3.

who practiced their monotheism as private individuals. By making service of God a public matter, he is recognized as the first person to accept God, not only as a transcendent being, but also as an intimate master who relates to His creation.[23]

> Rabbi Yohanan said in the name of Rabbi Simeon bar Yohai, 'From the day that the Holy One, blessed be He, created the world, there was no man who called the Holy One, blessed be He, Lord, until Abraham came and called Him Lord.'[24]

Abraham is also believed to have followed the entire Torah even though he neither received it nor was commanded to follow it.[25] Because the Torah is the blueprint for the world,[26] he was able to recognize his role in history and fulfill his purpose even without specific instructions. Since he was the one person who not only had the essential characteristics for chosenness but also had realized them for the fulfillment of God's goal in history even before being given the task, God's choice of Abraham could never be misunderstood as arbitrary.

Despite certain midrashim that portray the Jews in Egypt and during the exodus in a negative light, the Jews were not chosen based upon Abraham's merit alone. They, as opposed to any other descendent people, succeeded their ancestor in displaying the same attributes that allowed for God to approach Abraham in the first place. The sages interpret the verse, "He shone forth from Seir and appeared from the mountains of Paran,"[27] to mean that God first offered the Torah to all the other nations, who rejected it. Finally, God offered the Torah to the Israelites, who accepted it.[28] A superficial reading of the midrash supports a Rawlsian view of

---

[23] See *Tiferet Israel,* Chapter 19 by Rabbi Judah Loew.
[24] BT *Berakhot* 7b.
[25] BT *Yoma* 28b.
[26] *Genesis Rabbah* 1:1.
[27] Deuteronomy 33:2.
[28] BT *Avodah Zarah* 2b.

chosenness as being the outcome of natural chance or contingent on social circumstances[29] and therefore irrelevant as a distinctive factor in considering the requirements which define moral personality.[30] Yet since all nations evidently had the potential to become the chosen people by accepting the Torah, the idea that the Jewish people have an inherent differentiating moral propensity that justified God choosing them is revealed in the reasons for why the nations rejected the Torah. Upon being offered the Torah, the nations immediately inquired as to the nature of its obligations. In reply, God gave each nation a different example of the Torah's commandments. To the descendants of Esau, the example was the prohibition of murder, for the descendants of Ammon and Moab it was adultery, and for those descending from Ishmael it was robbery. Each nation justified its rejection of the Torah by claiming that the very example that God gave to represent the laws of the Torah was the action that defined them as a people.[31]

If God really intended to offer the Torah to the nations, why would He use as examples the very prohibitions that define them? Furthermore, the justification for rejecting the Torah based upon these prohibitions is groundless since the Noahide laws already prohibit such actions. The midrash wishes to demonstrate the singularity of the Jewish people, since not only did they not inquire as to the nature of the Torah's obligations but also they agreed to obey its more demanding mode of conduct. While God's choosing of the Jews made them the chosen people, the Jews' own character determined that choice.

The Vilna Gaon defends the idea of the intrinsic singularity of the Jewish people by interpreting the following Talmudic passage in light of the above midrash.

> The Elders of the House of Athens asked Rabbi Yehoshua ben Hananiah, 'If someone sought a woman's hand in

---

[29] *A Theory of Justice*, 11.
[30] *A Theory of Justice*, 445.
[31] *Sifrei Deuteronomy* 33.

> marriage and was refused, why would he go on to seek a woman of higher lineage?' Rabbi Yehoshua took a peg and thrust it into the bottom of the wall; it would not go in. He tried farther up, and it went in. 'It too has found its match,' he said.[32]

In reference to the manner in which the Torah was offered to the Jews, the Elders of the House of Athens argued that the Jewish people were God's last choice because they were the least preferred. The Vilna Gaon interprets Rabbi Yehoshua's symbolic response as saying that God wanted to bestow His wisdom to the entire world. Therefore, He first approached the nations that would have the greatest need for it. However, the encounter between God and the various nations revealed that none of the other nations was ready to receive the Torah. On the other hand, the Jewish people, who were most suitable to safeguard the Torah and execute God's will, were offered the Torah last due to the expectation that they would willingly accept it, which was confirmed by their response, "We will do and we will listen." Chosenness, according to this interpretation, does not signify favoritism but rather is the result of a unique proclivity the Jewish people have to accept upon themselves God's will.[33]

Rabbi Judah Halevi, whose path Rabbi Berkovits claims to follow,[34] advocates for the essential singularity of the Jewish people as strongly as Rabbi Berkovits denies it. Separating Adam's descendants into those who inherited Adam's perfection and receivability of the divine influence and those who did not, Rabbi Halevi traces the origins of the Jewish people from the directly descendent line of spiritually more attuned individuals.[35] In response to inquiry of the Khazar king as to why only the Jews were privileged to receive God's wisdom, Rabbi Halevi has the rabbi reply that not everyone is biologically fit to receive it. "The sons of

---

[32] BT *Bekhorot* 8b.

[33] See *The Juggler and the King*, Chapter 8.

[34] *God, Man and History*, 11.

[35] *The Kuzari*, 65.

Jacob were, however, distinguished from other people by godly qualities, which made them, so to speak, an angelic caste."[36] Their biological makeup allows for the divine influence to be received and the Torah to be kept.

Rabbi Mordechai Breuer, who shares Rabbi Berkovits's belief in the historical role of the Jewish people, disagrees with him regarding the necessity of human responsibility for being chosen. He describes the awesome difficulty involved in leaving one's homeland, birthplace, and ancestral home to a destination unbeknownst to him solely because of God's command, and argues that by his departure, Abraham not only submitted his reason to God's will but also overcame his own inertia in order to fulfill God's command. Thus he demonstrated that man's partnership with God in the process of creation includes also the founding of the chosen nation that will bring the telos of creation to fruition. He writes,

> Therefore, it was necessary that the ascent of Abraham [in becoming the patriarch of the chosen nation] was not done solely by the hands of God, like all other acts done in the world, rather [it must have been done] also by the hands of man. This is the acclaim of man, that he acts with free will in order to materialize the world's purpose. In this he is made a partner with God in the creation of the world, and not only that but it is as if the created's actions are greater than those of the Creator's, since the world was created by God without [actualization of its] final cause and necessary conclusion, and only man can bring the world's purpose to fruition, when he establishes God's house in God's land. He that concludes the story that is written in the book by [another] author – all goes after the conclusion. And until today [the people of] Israel are proud of their ancestor's actions, that he agreed to harness them to the chariot of God and become a chariot for the divine presence; and the

36 *The Kuzari*, 73.

> merit of this action of the forefather ascribes merit to his children until the end of days.[37]

Rabbi Breuer does not give man complete autonomy to actualize the world's potential, since "God does not create anything in vain" and if left solely in humankind's hands the telos of the world may come to just that effect. Rather, he maintains that although God's goal for history is necessarily embedded in its creation, His particular choice of Abraham could not have occurred without Abraham's choice as well.

Rabbi Berkovits's suggestion that the creation of the Jewish people is the consequence of God's choice and not recompense for proper action, either by the patriarchs or their descendants, has support from Rabbi Judah Loew of Prague's belief for the chosenness of the Jewish people. However, where Rabbi Berkovits maintains that the Jewish people "have been fashioned and formed through their national encounters with the Divine Presence,"[38] Rabbi Loew contends that the chosenness of Israel is part of the fabric of creation. In response to why the Torah does not mention Abraham's righteousness before he was given the command to go to the promised land, in contrast to the case of Noah where he was characterized as righteous before being commanded to build an ark, he writes,

> In Noah, the choice was particular, and a particular choice is according to the person and it is all according to the righteousness of his actions. In Abraham, however, it was not a particular choice; rather in the Israelite nation, which is his seed, as it is written regarding this choice 'and I will make you a great nation,' it is a universal choice, and a choice such as this does not depend upon [a person's] actions at all nor upon sin, because action is [something] particular [and not the essence of one's being]. Even though the merit of the patriarchs is beneficial;

---

[37] *Pirqe Bereshit*, 319.

[38] *God, Man and History*, 144

> nevertheless, the essence of the choice [does not depend upon it since it is] a universal choice in him and his seed.[39]

Because the chosenness of the Jewish people depends solely on God's will and not upon the merits of those chosen, they will remain the chosen people even if they temporarily disregard their divine mission. Chosenness is not a contingent characteristic but rather is part of the Jewish people's essence. Rabbi Loew gives three reasons for the essential chosenness of the Jewish people, which cannot be nullified. The first is that God's creation depends upon the Torah and the Torah must have a people to uphold it. Therefore, when God created the world He also gave, if only in thought until the actual conferral at Mount Sinai, the Torah to Israel. Once the Jewish people were designated as the keepers of the Torah, chosenness became a natural consequence. The second reason, which builds upon the first, is that God, who is One, needs a solitary first who can then influence the many. The third reason, which elucidates both why it must be Israel who are the upholders of the Torah and the solitary first who can dissipate God's influence to the world, is that God created Israel perfect in essence. Even if Israel sins, because their essence is perfect, temporary aberrations will neither effect their constitution nor their chosenness. Rabbi Loew's assertion that Israel was not chosen due to any action of their own does not achieve the same psychological perspective as Rabbi Berkovits's claim of arbitrary choice. Where Rabbi Berkovits's claim allows for one to dismiss any reason for why the Jewish people were chosen to direct one's attention to the obligations chosenness creates, Rabbi Loew's belief conflates the essence of the Jewish people and the characteristic of chosenness to give absolute weight to Jewish desert for being the chosen people.

The chosenness of the Jewish people, however, is not, as Jacob Katz describes it, "a difference in essence for which the individual

---

[39] *Netzah Israel*, Chapter 11.

was not responsible and over which he had no control."[40] As seen above in the biblical passage which gives the reasons for why God chose the Jewish people, it was not only due to their innate moral proclivity to which the covenant with the patriarchs alludes; God also loved the people themselves. In other words, the Jews have been chosen for a specific purpose in history that is different than the Gentiles, not arbitrarily but rather due to the moral proclivity of the Jewish people inherited from Abraham. This proclivity, however, means nothing unless it becomes manifest in the life of the Jewish people. Therefore, Jews are responsible both for the consequences of being chosen, through descent of Abraham, and for legitimating the choice by fulfilling the role for which they are chosen.

The dual reason for chosenness does not negate the legitimacy of conversion since it does not deny the existence of a similar potential moral proclivity in individual Gentiles, especially since Abraham is considered "the father of many nations." Therefore, as Menachem Kellner points out,[41] Maimonides does not distinguish between Jews and Gentiles with regards to the innate ability to attain prophecy and immortality as individuals, and he is able, as seen in his letter to Obadiah, to describe Abraham as the father of all converts. The difference between the individual Jew and the individual Gentile pre-conversion is the responsibility of actualizing one's Abrahamite moral potential.

Some, such as Rabbi Isaac Abravanel,[42] have taken Maimonides's wording in his thirteen principles, "When a man believes in all these fundamental principles, and his faith is thus clarified, he is then part of Israel whom we are to love, pity, and treat, as God commanded, with love and fellowship. Even if a Jew should commit every possible sin, out of lust or mastery by his

[40] *Tradition and Crisis*, 24.

[41] See *Maimonides on Judaism and the Jewish People*, Chapter 4.

[42] See his "Short Treatise Explaining the Secret of the Guide" and "Answers to Shaul ha-Kohen Ashkenazi." See also Arthur Hyman's "Thirteen Principles" in *Jewish Medieval and Renaissance Studies.*

lower nature, he will be punished for his sins but will still have a share in the world to come. He is one of the 'sinners in Israel.' But if a man gives up any one of these fundamental principles, he has removed himself from the Jewish community. He is an atheist, a heretic, an unbeliever who 'cuts among the plantings.' We are commanded to hate him and destroy him,"[43] to suggest that affirmation of the principles is what determines Israelite status. However, Maimonides's statement need not be understood as defining a Jew based upon doctrine. One could read the passage as simply referring to membership in the community of Israel without making mention of what comprises an individual Jew. A distinction between what constitutes a Jewish person and a Jewish community is also found in Rabbi Samson Raphael Hirsch where he writes,

> Wherever Jews who share the timeless Jewish loyalty to the Torah dwell in one locality, *they should unite of their own free will so that, together, they may preserve the Torah and translate it into living reality.* Even if there were only ten, or five, or even just two of them, *they would constitute the true Kehilla to whose loyal efforts God would look for the accomplishment of the Torah mission in that particular locality*...It is true that even those Jewish sons who have most openly deserted their calling and their irrevocable Jewish duty remain Jews nevertheless, just as, according to the basic principles of Judaism, even a baptized Jew remains a Jew. But a Jew can never form one religious community with baptized Jews, or regard as his own a community or communal institutions established and administered by and for baptized Jews.[44]

The idea that Maimonides distinguishes between what constitutes an individual Jew and a member of the Jewish community is further supported in Maimonides's halakhic decisions where he makes frequent reference to membership in the Jewish community and not to the essence of Jewish personhood, which he does not alter from

[43] *A Maimonides Reader*, 422.
[44] *Collected Writings* VI, 81.

the classic hereditary definition of being the progeny of a Jewish mother or through undergoing proper conversion. An example of how Maimonides differentiates between Jews who have left the Jewish community and Gentiles is seen in *Hilkhot Rotzeah u-Shemirat Nefesh*, where he writes that it is a mitzvah to kill *minim* and *apikorsim* who commit idolatry but not a Gentile who commits idolatry during times of peace.[45] If Maimonides believed that ideology truly determined Jewish personhood, then this distinction would not be consistent with that idea.

In describing the Jewish people as a collective versus Gentiles as a collective, Maimonides does portray a sense of Jewish superiority based both upon descent from Abraham and possession of the Torah, which, I believe, can be restated in terms of an Abrahamite moral proclivity[46] and its manifestation in action.[47] Abrahamic descent is not enough; rather, it is the source of responsibility and the reason for chosenness as a people. One must recognize the responsibility chosenness entails and thereby legitimate the choice by accepting the obligation of Torah observance.

With namesakes that signify their iconoclastic position[48] and their ultimate theological triumph,[49] the Jewish people must

---

[45] *Hilkhot Rotzeah u-Shemirat Nefesh*, 4:10–11.

[46] See Maimonides's Epistle to Yemen, where he writes regarding Israel's chosenness, "This did not happen because of our merits, but rather as an act of divine grace, and on account of our forefathers who were cognizant of God and submitted to Him…." (*A Maimonides Reader*, 439)

[47] See *Hilkhot Teshuva* 2:10, where he writes, "It is forbidden for one to be cruel and refuse to be appeased. One should rather be forgiving and slow to anger, and whenever a sinner asks for forgiveness one should grant it wholeheartedly and with a willing spirit. Even if the sinner had distressed him and sinned against him considerably, one should not seek revenge or bear a grudge. This is the path of the seed of Israel and their upright spirit. In contrast, the insensitive Gentiles do not act in this manner. Rather, their wrath is preserved forever. Concerning the Gibeonites, who did not forgive and refused to be appeased, it has been said, 'The Gibeonites were not of the Children of Israel.'"

[48] *Genesis Rabbah* 42:13. "And he told Abraham, the Ivri." Rabbi Yehuda said [that the word 'Ivri' means that] the whole world was on one side and he was on the other.

recognize that they have the inherent ability to accomplish their historical function. To believe that the Jewish people were put in a position of such magnitude solely because someone had to fill the role both demeans the character of the Jewish people and dishonors the position itself. How are the Jewish people to have any courage of conviction when the nations of the world declare that they disregard the contemporary mores of humanity!? How much more difficult is it for the solitary exilic Jew to defend himself against his neighbors!? Without self-confidence, the authentic Jew will undoubtedly begin to justify himself vis-à-vis his surroundings and accommodate his beliefs to conform to the society in which he lives. It is only natural that those who lack a strong sense of self would surrender that selfhood in order to find definition as part of a group. Yet Abraham had the confidence to know that although he was but dust and ashes, his opinion had to be heard if it could possibly influence a proper conclusion. The Jewish people are chosen because they inherited Abraham's spiritual and psychological strength of character, and an authentic Jew should be one who recognizes that fact.

The Land of Israel

In Rabbi Berkovits's philosophy of history, the importance of the land of Israel is based upon its efficacy in allowing the Jewish people to bring the purpose of history to fruition. In other words, it is the chosen land because it is the land of the chosen people.

> If… the people of Israel is the instrument of realization, there must be a land of Israel as the place of realization. There must be a place on earth in which the people are in command of their own destiny, where the comprehensive public deed of Judaism may be enacted.[50]

According to this premise, any land where the Jewish people could create a sovereign society would suffice and could therefore take

---

[49] Genesis 32:29.
[50] *Essential Essays*, 182.

the place of the land of Israel. Given his conception of halakhic development, even the agricultural commandments would not preclude another land from being the place where the Jewish people could fulfill their destiny, since, especially in today's nonagricultural society, Jews could still show the world how to create a God-centered republic without specific agricultural obligations.[51] Although the land of Israel is the preferred place for a Jewish state for nostalgic reasons, the choice ultimately depends on the efficacy of a given land, since, in the long run, practicality is more effective than emotions in creating change. The land of Israel's importance depends on its ability to create a productive environment for the Jewish people to fulfill their mission; if the land cannot create such an environment it will not maintain the same significance.

The idea that the land of Israel plays a contingent role in the definition of the Jewish people was expounded by Rabbi Samson Raphael Hirsch. Building upon Rabbi Saadia Gaon's belief that the Jewish people are a nation only by virtue of the Torah,[52] Rabbi Hirsch distinguishes the Jewish people from other nations in that where other nations develop by virtue of the land upon which they live, Israel develops only through its attachment to the Torah. He writes,

> Israel should be one nation, an entire nation that should have no other foundation for its existence, survival, activity and significance than this Torah. It is to see the realization and devoted observance of this God-given 'fiery Law' as its one contribution in world history for the edifice of human salvation…Nay more, Israel is a nation that became a nation only through and for the Torah, a nation that once owned a land and existed as a state only through and for the Torah, and which possessed that land and that statehood only as instruments for translating the Torah into living reality. This is why Israel was a people even before it

[51] See Rabbi Berkovits's position regarding repealing the laws of *shemittah* below.

[52] *Beliefs and Opinions*, 158.

> possessed land and statehood; this, too, is why Israel survived as a people even after its land was destroyed and its statehood lost, and this is why it will survive as a nation as long as it does not lose this only *morasha*, this sole foundation for its survival and significance.[53]

The nation of Israel, according to Rabbi Hirsch, will exist within any historical environment as long as the focus of its historical mission is in tact. Whether in the land of Israel or in a different land, the Jewish people are a people when they carry out the precept of the Torah.

Although Rabbi Hirsch negates the importance of the land of Israel in terms of its contribution towards defining the nation of Israel, he does not advocate a position where the value of the land of Israel is solely dependent upon the efficacy of Jewish practice in the land. Rather, just as God chose the nation of Israel to fulfill the mission of educating the world in reaching its telos, the land of Israel was chosen as the first place for that mission to be fulfilled.

> When the Lord apportioned the regions of the earth among men, He retained for Himself, for a special purpose, one land *Eretz Israel*, the Land of the Jews, which was to serve as the soil for His Law and of His people which was to live for the fulfillment of His Law. And within this one land He reserved for a special purpose one place, the Holy Mountain, to serve as the abode for the Sanctuary of His Law. From this place He would proclaim His presence and it was from this place, too, that the Law with its hallowing force was to win over, first Israel and then all the other nations of the world for God and for His Law.[54]

The fact that the nation of Israel and the land of Israel do not have a reciprocal relationship of definition, common in many modern nationalistic ideologies, does not take away from either Israel as a nation or the land. Rather, the relationship, as Rabbi Hirsch

---

[53] *Collected Writings* VIII, 35.

[54] *Chapters of the Fathers*, 116.

describes it, between the people and its land gives importance to each per se and validates both even when that relationship is estranged.

Rabbi Hirsch is not the only one to argue that the land of Israel has import in and of itself. The sages describe the relationship between God, the Jewish people, and the land of Israel in the following terms:

> The land of Israel is beloved since the Holy One, blessed by He, chose it. You find that when God created the world He distributed the various lands to the heavenly ministers and chose the land of Israel for Himself.... He also chose the people of Israel as His portion.... Said the Holy One, blessed be He, 'Let Israel, who became My portion, inherit the Land which became My portion.'[55]

The sages clearly state, contrary to Rabbi Berkovits's theory that the land is subordinate to the Jewish people in importance, that the land of Israel was chosen in its own right, equal in importance to the Jewish people. Inheriting the land of Israel is portrayed as a privilege and not an entitlement. If the Jewish people do not live up to their divine expectations, they are no longer permitted to receive God's portion. As the Torah stipulates, "You shall faithfully observe all My laws and all My regulations, lest the land to which I bring you to settle spew you out."[56] God clearly promised the patriarchs that the land would belong to their descendants forever,[57] yet the promise neither disregarded the significance of the land in its own right nor the recognition and respect that it deserves.

Rabbi Berkovits's claim that he is the modern successor to Rabbi Judah Halevi falls short in relation to his conception of the land of Israel as well. In his explanation to the king of the Khazars for why he wishes to immigrate to Israel, the rabbi mentions that he

---

[55] *Midrash Tanhuma,* Re'eh 8.
[56] Leviticus 20:22.
[57] Genesis 13:15.

seeks to free himself from the service of those whose favor he will never win, which could seemingly be the basis for a sovereignty-oriented theory for the value of the land of Israel. However, the context of his response demonstrates his belief that the land is significant per se and is important to individual Jews, not only a sovereign Jewish community. After detailing the special character of the land of Israel, both in terms of its natural preeminence and ensuing regulation,[58] the king of the Khazars still inquires as to why the rabbi seeks to immigrate. He asks, "What can be sought in Palestine nowadays, since the divine reflex is absent from it, while, with a pure mind and desire, one can approach God in any place? Why wilt thou run into danger on land and water and among various peoples?"[59] The rabbi answers that one's heart and soul can only be perfect in the land especially chosen by God. Therefore, if one truly desires to serve Him, he will seek to connect himself to the land. When immigration is impossible, continual engrossment through prayer and supplication suffices, yet if one is able, he must endeavor to serve God in the land that He has chosen.[60]

The practical ramification between whether the land of Israel is important in and of itself or whether this importance depends upon Jewish sovereignty plays a significant role in the authentic Jew's perspective on what his relationship to the land should be. On the statement in the Talmud that one who lives outside the land of Israel is considered as if he were an idol worshipper, Rabbi Berkovits comments that "it links the importance of the land not so much to the Jew as to the realization of Judaism."[61] The reason he is considered as an idol worshipper is not because he has idolatrous beliefs but because he cannot perform the actions of Judaism in the ideal manner, as part of an autonomous Jewish community. His interpretation begs the question of what would be a better secondary alternative – to live in a large semi-autonomous Jewish

---

[58] *The Kuzari,* Book 2.
[59] *The Kuzari,* 293.
[60] *The Kuzari,* 293–295.
[61] *Essential Essays*, 179.

community outside the land of Israel or to live in the land of Israel alone amongst Gentiles. If the importance of the land of Israel is not essential but only as a means for the public practice of Judaism, it would seem that living among Jews would be the better choice due to the greater ability to practice Judaism in a fuller manner. The Talmud, on the other hand, states that the importance of living in the land of Israel is greater than living among other Jews.

> Our Rabbis taught: One should always live in the land of Israel, even in a town most of whose inhabitants are idolaters, but let no one live outside the land, even in a town most of whose inhabitants are Jews; for whoever lives in the land of Israel may be considered to have a God, but whoever lives outside the land may be regarded as one who has no God. For it is said in Scripture, 'To give you the land of Canaan, to be your God.' Has he, then, who does not live in the land, no God? But [this is what the text intended] to tell you, that whoever lives outside the Land may be regarded as one who worships idols.[62]

The Talmudic commentators explain that only the land of Israel has God's direct attention, while all other lands are influenced by the celestial powers. Therefore, a Jew living outside the land of Israel has a spiritual impediment that interferes in his relationship with the divine. It is not the inability to perform the commandments as public deeds within a sovereign Jewish community that distances him from God, but rather the place where he has performed them.

The sages defend the importance of the land of Israel in their statement about the performance of commandments in exile. On the partial verse, "And you will soon perish from the good land,"[63] the sages remark, "Although I banish you from the land to [live in] the Diaspora, make yourselves distinctive by the commandments so that when you return they shall not be novelties to you. This can be compared to a master who, angry with his wife, sends her back to

---

[62] BT *Ketubbot* 110b.
[63] Deuteronomy 11:17.

her father's house, telling her, 'Adorn yourself with precious things, so that when you come back they will not be novelties to you.'"[64] The passage indicates that in addition to their intrinsic value, commandments performed in exile serve a twofold secondary function. They prevent assimilation and they remind Jews of how they should act once they have returned to the land of Israel. No matter how scrupulously performed they may be, the commandments in exile do not fulfill the function for which they were originally intended. Just as the adornments that a banished wife wears in her father's house do not please her husband but only encourage her to seek reconciliation and keep the dynamics of their relationship fresh in her mind, so too the commandments performed in exile can only help to demonstrate the Jewish people's willingness to have a direct relationship with God in His land.

In light of the understanding that one can only fulfill one's obligation ideally by living in the land of Israel, we can understand the rabbinic dictum that dwelling in the land of Israel is of equal importance to observing all the commandments of the Torah.[65] When we compare this statement to its analogue that learning Torah is equal to all the other commandments, we see that the relationship of the Jewish people to the land of Israel and to the Torah is the same. While both are of inestimable value in and of themselves, they also serve the Jewish people in recognizing who they are. On a superficial level, the analogy is that just as a Jew cannot perform a commandment properly without knowing how to do so, he also cannot perform it properly outside of God's land. On a different level, the parallel could be that just as learning the Torah for its own sake strengthens one's relationship with God, so does simply living in the land of Israel. The authentic Jew realizes that living in the land of Israel is not just a requirement for an autonomous Jewish society; it is also an obligation incumbent upon

---

[64] *Sifrei* Ekev, 43.

[65] *Sifrei* Re'eh, 80; Tosefta *Avodah Zarah* 5:3.

him as an individual Jew.[66] Once Jews become aware of this personal connection, even those who live in the Diaspora will become more sensitive and proactive towards issues relating to the land of Israel.

Exile

The idea that the Jewish people are in exile because of their sins is not just a meekly-worded text recited during prayer, but rather a firm belief that the Jewish tradition has held for centuries. One need not go any further than the first pages of the Talmud to understand how ingrained the association between sin and exile is in Jewish consciousness. In determining the appropriate time to recite the *Shema,* Rabbi Eliezer states that one has until the end of the first watch to recite. He purposely uses the terminology of watches instead of hours, though its ambiguity may result in misinterpretation, solely to make allusion to the corresponding

---

[66] Nahmanides, in his Addendum to Maimonides's *Book of Commandments*, counts living in the land of Israel, even during the exile, as one of the 613 biblically prescribed commandments. The Megillat Esther claims that Maimonides did not count living in the land of Israel as one of the 613 because it does not apply during the time of the exile. However, Maimonides writes, "At all times, a person should dwell in the land of Israel" (*Hilkhot Melakhim* 5:12), indicating that he believes that the obligation is in effect even during the exile. A possible explanation for Maimonides's reason for not counting it as one of the 613 commandments may not be because the obligation is contingent on the Temple's existence; rather, as he states in his tenth foundation for the counting of the commandments, he does not count as an independent commandment a requirement for the fulfillment of another commandment. Because the ideal fulfillment of the commandments can only take place in the land of Israel, living in the land of Israel is a prerequisite and therefore cannot be counted as an independent commandment. The Tosafists (BT *Ketubbot* 110b) exempt people from the obligation of living in the land of Israel because of the danger of travel and the lack of knowledge of how to perform commandments that involve the land itself. By giving auxiliary reasons for why the obligation is not in effect, the Tosafists recognize that the obligation exists even during exile, it just cannot be put into practice due to extenuating circumstances. Later authorities dismiss the Tosafists' reasons and recognize the obligation to live in the land of Israel even during exile. See *Pithei Teshuva* on *Even ha-Ezer* 75:6, *Teshuvot Maharit* 2:28, and *Shnei Luhot ha-Brit* 1:75b for further information.

watches in Heaven. He makes the allusion to remind everyone that "at each watch the Holy One, blessed be He, sits and roars like a lion and says, 'Woe to the children on account of whose sins I destroyed My house and burned My temple and exiled them among the nations of the world.'"[67] Elsewhere in the Talmud, the sages declare that exile atones for the Jewish people's sins,[68] yet they disagree to what extent exile alone expiates without any action on the sinner's part.[69] Rather than enabling it to come to fruition, exile is considered to be so injurious to the history of the Jewish people that the sages comment that it is one of the four things God repents having created.[70]

The idea that exile, in the absolute sense, cannot be a primary intention for the fulfillment of Israel's divine mission can be seen through the explanation of the Mishna which states, "exile comes into the world because of idolatry, and sexual immorality, and bloodshed, and for [not observing] the Sabbatical year."[71] Analysis of this Mishna must be divided into two parts, whereby the first explanation of exile is the three cardinal sins and the second explanation is for not observing the Sabbatical year. With regard to the first explanation, Halakha differentiates between whether an individual – or in certain cases a singular Jewish community – performs these crimes or if the Jewish people as a whole perform them. In the case of an individual, the penalty for willing performance is death,[72] yet in the case of the people as a whole it is exile. Furthermore, the Bible records three societies that were destroyed as punishment for committing acts of idolatry, sexual immorality, and bloodshed; namely, the generation of the Flood, the people of Sodom, and Egypt. Through our investigation,

---

[67] BT *Berakhot* 3a.
[68] BT *Berakhot* 56a.
[69] BT *Sanhedrin* 37b.
[70] BT *Sukkah* 52b.
[71] Mishna *Avot* 5:11.
[72] See *Hilkhot Avodat Kokhavim* 3:1 and 4:6, *Hilkhot Issurei Biah* 1:1, *Hilkhot Rotzeah* 1:1.

hopefully we can be able to understand how these sins demand eradication of the sinner and how exile is an exceptional transposition given on account of the necessity of the Jewish people's fulfillment of their divine mission.

The performance of the three cardinal sins and their ensuing punishment must be considered in light of the statement by Rabbi Shimon ha-Tzaddik, "On three things the world stands – on Torah, on *Avodah*, and on deeds of kindness."[73] The question that begs to be asked is should not the statement read that man exists on account of these three things instead of the world? Man's composition is such that his perception and recognition of both himself and others is intrinsically tied to his being in the world; he does not perceive the world outside of his influence upon it and its influence upon him. The idea that the world was created for the sake of man means that neither man nor the world can exist without the other; both are intrinsically tied to the other's existence. Therefore, the explanation of the statement by Rabbi Shimon ha-Tzaddik must be seen through the following perspective: the world was created for the sake of goodness, as we see continually in the first chapter of Genesis, "God saw that it was good". Were it not for this goodness, there would be no justification for the world. Except for a very small percentage of the population, no one can be completely good. This is a fundamental element of our being; we have inclinations towards both good and evil and even when our intentions are seemingly good we sometimes are not able to differentiate between our intentions or foresee the consequences of our goodly-intended actions, as King Solomon states, "For there is not a righteous man upon earth, that does good, and sins not."[74] Although it is impossible for a particular individual to maintain a complete adherence to the good, an interdependent community is able to uphold the standard of goodness requisite for the upkeep of the world. Where individuals are lacking in the absolute, each

---

[73] Mishna *Avot* 1:2.
[74] Ecclesiastes 7:20.

individual has a propensity for particular areas of goodness. A community, which is an amalgamation of a number of individuals, all who have certain propensities to certain areas of goodness, whereby each individual can give support to another's lacking, is able to adhere to the ideal of goodness, thus legitimating the world's creation.

Even though there is a prohibition for non-Jews to study the Torah, this only refers to those commandments that do not pertain to them; however if Torah is taken in reference to what does pertain to them, the seven commandments for all humanity, then the learning of Torah is not only a requirement so they act correctly, but its study for its own sake is something to be praised. "Rabbi Meir used to say: Whence do we know that even a non-Jew who studies the Torah is as a High Priest? From the verse, 'which, if man do, he shall live in them.' Priests, Levites, and Israelites are not mentioned, but men: hence thou may learn that even a non-Jew who studies the Torah is as a High Priest! — That refers to their own seven laws."[75] The Torah is what differentiates man from beast; it is the source of a wisdom that is not tied to instinctual motivations but rather attempts to transform man's mental capacity into one that rises above his material circumstances. It is a source to discover the good for which the world was created, and through the rigors of its study, it will refashion man in terms of that good.

Avodah can be seen in two respects. The first is occupation, to be a productive entity. Man was created in the image of God and just as God created the world, man, too, is a creative being. Whereas animals produce out of necessity, either through instinct or as a means to sustain themselves (the two are interrelated), man produces creatively, with consciousness towards the product of his creation. Just as God created so that the world will be good, to be in partnership with Him, man must also create with focus on the good.

---

[75] BT *Sanhedrin* 59a.

The second interpretation of *Avodah* is service. Recognizing one's own imperfections and inadequacies as compared to the capacity of both God and the community, man becomes humble and submissive, yearning for an intimate relationship with God and with his fellow man in order to overcome his sense of incompleteness and insufficiency. Through man's service, he will join in relationship with God and become part of a community. Man, within a religious community, becomes intimate with God by acting for Him. He also creates bonds with other people in promoting common goals.

Man's awareness that he is not alone demands that he recognize others. Because he lives within a social matrix, reciprocity is a consequence of interdependence. Cooperation is the only way to achieve both one's individual and communal potential, for, as we have seen above, it is only through cooperation that a person and a community can become whole. With regard to communal interdependence the sages remark, "In three respects are acts of kindness superior to charity: charity can be done only with one's money, but acts of kindness can be done with one's person and one's money. Charity can be given only to the poor, acts of kindness both to the rich and the poor. Charity can be given to the living only, acts of kindness can be done both to the living and to the dead [by attending to their funeral and burial]."[76] Giving to others altruistically, because they are human, in turn reveals one's own humanity. Mutual recognition of humanness allows men to collaborate for the benefit of society and to self-actualize through cooperation towards collective self-improvement.

These three pillars make up the foundation which is called good. God's continuous creation and maintenance of the world lasts only as long as He can recognize the good that the world contains, as emphasized in the approval of the creation process. However, when the good is not realized, the foundation upon which the world rests crumbles and its very reason of existence

---

[76] BT *Sukkah* 49b.

becomes for naught. In this situation, the world loses its own justification and risks its own dissolution.

In metaphysics as in physics, every action has an equal yet opposite reaction, and the three pillars on which the world stands – Torah, *Avodah*, and deeds of kindness – have three opposing forces that can break the foundation and destroy the world. Against the pillar of Torah, which trains the intellect and makes man distinct, is sexual immorality, which is compared to the actions of animals. Animals rarely maintain monogamous relationships and sexual activity is an instinctual experience. As stated above, the main difference between humans and their animal counterparts exist in the ability to prioritize and retain a hierarchy of desires. His humanness stems from his capacity to consider his being. Furthermore, man not only has consideration for his own physical health; he also has concern for his social well-being through his relationship with others. His hierarchy of desires is what gives him restraint; it controls his basest, most instinctual desires in order to promote the betterment of his being.

Allusion to the analogy of sexual immorality to acts of animals is made with regards to the offering of a woman suspected of an adulterous relationship. Having relations with someone other than her husband nullifies the relationship aspect of intercourse, because intercourse becomes a means of gratification of desire, similar to an animal instinct, and not a manifestation of the bonds of matrimony. The distinction between human and animal has dissipated because the intellect has been subdued by bodily desire.

Against *Avodah* is idolatry. The prohibition against idolatry is twofold, performing the particular acts prescribed to be directed toward God for the sake of idols and performing acts particular to specific idols.[77] We can understand this twofold prohibition in terms of the different interpretations we gave for *Avodah* above. Regarding *Avodah* in terms of man's productive activity, if man would act in the same manner as would be proper yet has perverted

[77] *Hilkhot Avodat Kokhavim* 3:2–3.

the subject toward which he is directed, he has transformed his action into a manner of idolatry. No longer does he imitate God because God is no longer his focus; rather, he has forsaken the partnership in improving the world and through his actions has facilitated its demise. Similarly, when one is acting towards a specific idol in the particular ritual that it requires, one is, in effect, fulfilling his desire for completion via a relationship, not with God and His community but with an idol and those who adhere to falsity. He envelopes himself in inauthenticity; the society he has chosen, and therefore its actions, language and values mask the person's true self. He recognizes his being only through the false concepts of his society and does not have the tools with which to discover what he has buried within himself. The world in which he lives, seen through his delusory perception, is as artificial as he is. He has destroyed the truth of the world, simply because he has destroyed the truth of himself.

Theft[78] and murder are both said to contradict acts of kindness, yet there is no disagreement in its meta-analysis. Seen in its narrow definition, in acts of kindness one gives of himself and by theft one takes from another; acts of kindness help people live and murder takes away that life. On a meta-scale, the idea behind acts of kindness, as seen above, is the recognition of another as a human, an equal member of one's world. Giving of oneself does not diminish what one has, because all is shared through the process of mutual relationships. What one gains, on the contrary, is of infinite value, mutual recognition of each other's humanness. Theft, and murder as its ultimate extreme, views another, not as a subject of mutual recognition, but as an object from which to extract utility. It is a denial of the humanness of another, and, in return, an inability to recognize the humanness in oneself. Without the perception of the human, the world loses its function, since, as we have seen, the world and the human are intertwined both in terms of creation and purpose.

---

[78] See Rabbi Judah Loew's *Derekh Hayyim* 1:2.

Recognizing the deleterious capabilities of sexual immorality, idolatry, and theft – of both body and property, at least according to Rabbi Meir[79] – the rabbis advised that one should let himself be killed rather than commit one of these acts, even if due to compulsion. The sacrifice of the person, so as not to commit even a coerced action, demonstrates the power of the acts in and of themselves, not just the force of the intentions behind them. Even when coercion is proof of lack of malintent, a person must refuse to commit such sins, for fear of the possible consequence of risking the foundation upon which the world stands. How much more can we understand the consequences of the three societies who partook in these actions intentionally and voluntarily!

The Talmud indicates that the destruction of the First Temple, and the ensuing exile, was the consequence of the practice of idolatry, immorality, and bloodshed.[80] Based upon the Halakha regarding individuals who commit these sins and the three societies who engaged in them, as well as the theological justification for the consequences of commission, it would seem evident that the destruction of the Temple and the exile was an act of mercy which replaced the true deserved punishment. In fact, such is the explanation given for why Asaf sang instead of lamented when describing the destruction of the Temple, "I am singing because God vented His wrath upon wood and stone and did not vent his wrath upon Israel."[81] Rabbi Bahya ben Asher gives reason for why God decreed exile instead of destruction for the Jewish people. He writes,

> As it says, 'For I Hashem do not change, and you, sons of Jacob, are not consumed.' The explanation is just as it is impossible that My name would change so is it impossible that Israel would be consumed. And because Israel should have been destroyed for their sins, yet it is impossible for

---

[79] BT *Ketubbot* 19a.

[80] BT *Yoma* 9b.

[81] *Lamentations Rabbah* 4:15.

> them to be consumed, so it was decreed upon them that they would be dispersed and subjected among the nations.[82]

For this reason, one could understand Rabbi Judah Loew's contention that although the sins of idolatry, immorality, and bloodshed caused the exile, there must be a meta-cause as the punishment does not fit the crime. He answers that it is only due to the relationship between God and the Jewish people that would allow for such an exception.[83]

The power of not observing the Sabbatical year to cause exile is inherent to the meaning of the commandment itself. As aforementioned, God chose the land of Israel as His portion on earth just as He chose the Jewish people to be his first-born children. The law commanding the Jewish people to allow the land to lie fallow gives acknowledgment that the Jewish people are neither the owners nor the product of the land. Like Adam, the Jewish people were placed upon the land to work and guard it. Fulfilling the commandment of the Sabbatical year thus demonstrates that the Jewish people recognize that their destiny is in carrying out God's will, while disregarding the law conveys a denial of God's supreme authority over the earth and mankind. Therefore, when the Sabbatical year is not observed, God must demonstrate that the relationship between the nation and the land upon which it lives is not intrinsic but rather due to mutual necessity in the service of God.

While we have shown how exile must be a consequence of sin without primacy of legitimacy in the absolute sense with respect to the exile after the destruction of the First Temple, it is now necessary to discuss the consequence of exile in relation to the destruction of the Second Temple. The Talmud records a discussion as to why the Second Temple was destroyed:

---

[82] *Kad ha-Kemah*, Geula.
[83] *Netzah Israel*, Chapter 2.

> But why was the Second Temple destroyed, seeing that in its time they were occupying themselves with Torah, [observance of] commandments, and the practice of charity? Because therein prevailed hatred without cause. That teaches you that groundless hatred is considered as of even gravity with the three sins of idolatry, immorality, and bloodshed.[84]

The idea that baseless hatred of one's fellow is equal in measure to the three cardinal sins allows for the admission that exile after the destruction of the Second Temple must be seen in the same light as after the destruction of the First. However, the idea of equality of magnitude between them must still be explained. Rabbi Solomon ben Aderet justifies the comparison by explaining that the perspective of the one who performs these acts and the one who bears this hatred is the same.[85] Hatred implies a rejection and distancing from the object of focus; it breaks any relationship of mutual respect and recognition. To harbor hatred without any external cause would therefore be a willing internalization of focus without any concern for the world. Anything external to the person would be perceived as an object to be used and not a subject with which to relate. Such is also the perspective of a murderer, an idolater, and one who engages in sexual immorality.

Rabbi Hasdai Crescas understands the nature of the current exile, and thereby the relationship between baseless hatred and the three cardinal sins, in a related but not identical manner. He writes that the current exile is still a remnant of the exile to Babylon. In Ezra's time there was not a complete redemption since Cyrus, and in later years other monarchies, maintained control over politics in Israel. The Jewish people, upon the return from the Babylonian exile, were able to remove their inclination for idolatry and sexual

---

[84] BT *Yoma* 9b.

[85] *Perush ha-Aggadot le-Rashba*, Siman 368.

immorality to become manifest in their life,[86] yet they did not remove the psychological foundation upon which those sins are able to base themselves. Therefore, Titus was able to destroy the Second Temple, ending the quasi-redemption they were able to achieve.[87] Based upon the idea that "any generation in which the Temple is not rebuilt is considered as if they had destroyed it," it becomes clear how the psychological perspective of baseless hatred is as powerful as the three cardinal sins. Just as God created the world *ex nihilo*, yet continues to preserve its existence, so do the three cardinal sins return the world to naught while baseless hatred carries on the destruction.

There does seem to be a minority opinion about the exile which Rabbi Berkovits could possibly have used to support his claim.

> Rabbi Eleazar also said: The Holy One, blessed be He, did not exile Israel among the nations except so that converts might join them, for it is said, 'And I will sow her unto Me in the land.' Surely a man sows a *se'ah* in order to harvest many *kor*! While Rabbi Yohanan deduced [the same idea] from this, 'And I will have compassion upon her that has not obtained compassion.'[88]

However, when one examines this passage within the greater context of the discussion, he will conclude that the views of Rabbi Eleazar and Rabbi Yohanan agree with the general belief concerning the reason for exile. The Talmudic discussion in which this passage occurs relates to understanding God's prophecy to Hosea. After witnessing the sins committed by his fellow Israelites, Hosea proposes to God that He exchange the Jews for another people. Through his command to Hosea to marry a harlot, have

[86] BT *Yoma* 69b.
[87] *Or Hashem*, Maamar 3, Helek 1, Clal 8, Chapter 2. See Rabbi Samson Raphael Hirsch's *Nineteen Letters*, Letter 9, which also states that the Second Temple period was only a reunion for the purpose of reinforcing the Jewish people's connection to the Torah before they would endeavor the long exile that awaited them.
[88] BT *Pesahim* 87b.

children with her, and then separate from her, God shows Hosea that He could never abandon the Jewish people no matter how unfaithful they might be. Rabbi Eleazar then declares that even when the Holy One, blessed be He, is angry, He remembers compassion, supporting his statement with a verse that directly alludes to Hosea's advice and God's response to it. This statement immediately precedes his remark regarding the exile and therefore puts his view of it in that perspective. The juxtaposition of Rabbi Eleazar's two statements provides the reason for Rabbi Samuel Eliezer Edeles's explanation that if God desired merely to punish the Jewish people, He could have used any other punishment. It is because God does not punish without also showing compassion and conferring teleological benefit that He decided upon exile.[89] The simple meaning of Rabbi Yohanan's proof-text is that God will forgive the Jewish people for their sins and renew His loving relationship with them. Rabbi Yohanan changes the simple meaning of the verse to refer to the nations of the world, who are compassionately given the opportunity, through Israel's exile, to recognize God. Because Rabbi Yohanan's statement is subordinate to Rabbi Eleazar's, it is understood that he shares the idea that exile must serve a positive purpose and not be solely a punishment for sin. Citing the same verse to prove their positions, Rabbi Eleazar uses the first part of the verse to allude to the Jewish people's dispersion among the nations, while Rabbi Yohanan cites the second part of the verse to explain how the dispersion is beneficial. Neither Rabbi Eleazar nor Rabbi Yohanan, however, believes that exile serves only the purpose of proselytization and is therefore an intrinsic part of the Jewish people's teleological history.

The idea of exile as having a secondary purpose of incorporating the nations of the world into the service of the divine while its cause still being punishment for a previous sin is expanded

[89] See Maharsha on BT *Pesahim* 87b.

upon by Rabbi Bahya ben Asher. Given that we have seen above his contention that Israel was exiled because it could not have been destroyed, he gives two further reasons for why they were dispersed among the nations.

> The reason for their dispersion, in my opinion, is for two reasons. First, in order to spread Israel to all ends among the nations, who lack understanding, so that they will teach the nations about belief in the existence of God, may He be blessed, and in the matter of divine providence which influences men individually. The second reason is that Israel sinned in the holy land, which is the focal point of the world…thus it was decreed upon them that they would be exiled to the ends of the earth, i.e. the nethermost points, measure for measure…[90]

The idea of Israel's exile serving a positive teleological purpose is also adopted by Rabbi Hayyim ben Betzalel,[91] brother of Rabbi Judah Loew, and Rabbi Samson Raphael Hirsch, among others.

Rabbi Berkovits's claim that exile defines the constitution of the Jewish people comes from his reading of God's first command to Abraham and the covenant between the pieces. According to his reading, Abraham's departure from his father's house and God's statement that his descendants would be strangers in a land not their own symbolizes how God's people cannot rest until He is universally recognized. They must live in exile so as to identify with the exile of the Divine Presence.

> The call that went out to Abraham was a call for identification with the divine plan in history. But by way of this identification with the divine purpose and the divine Galut, he became Abraham, the father of a 'multitude of nations.' The Egyptian exile was of similar significance for his descendants….[92]

---

[90] *Kad ha-Kemah*, Geula.
[91] *Sefer ha-Hayyim*, Geula ve-Yeshua, Chapter 7.
[92] *Crisis and Faith*, 155.

However, his reading of the accounts seems to contradict the popular understanding of the exile of the Divine Presence, since the Divine Presence is usually thought to have accompanied the Jews into exile and not the other way around. It also seems to differ with the simple reading of Abraham's encounters with God.

It is true that God's command to Abraham caused him to leave his country, his birthplace, and his father's house. Such a departure would normally be thought of as exile, for who can perceive separating oneself from family and friends as anything else? Yet the emphasis of the command is not on Abraham's leaving but on where he is going. If the Torah were to stress Abraham's departure, the verb used in the sentence would be צא or עזב. The verb לך means to go somewhere, directing one's attention to the destination rather than the departure. God's command should therefore be read, "Go for yourself to the land that I will show you, even if you must leave what you already know, for your journey culminates in blessing and there you will become a great nation." Rather than starting with exile, Abraham's identification with the divine purpose commences with redemption.

Contrary to Rabbi Berkovits, Nahmanides explains that the covenant between the pieces foretold not the teleological requirement of exile but rather that it is a consequence of sin. Consonant with the rabbinic interpretation that the prophecy alludes to the four exiles of the Jewish people, Nahmanides equates the causes of those exiles with the exile explicitly under discussion.

> The experience came to Abraham because when the Holy One, blessed be He, made a covenant with him to give the land to his children as an everlasting possession, He said to him, by way of a residuary of His gift, that during the four exiles the nations would subjugate his children and rule in their land, subject to the condition that they sin before Him. Following the general allusion, He then informed him explicitly concerning another exile into which they will first

> go, namely, the Egyptian exile with which he had already been punished.[93]

According to Nahmanides, Abraham sinned by taking his wife, Sarah, to Egypt during the time of famine and exposing her to danger instead of staying in the land and trusting in God to provide.[94] Even though his sin was inadvertent, his lax attitude towards the land and his readiness to go to Egypt served to be the impetus for the Jewish peoples' exilic sojourning, which began with their descent to Egypt during a famine as well.

Nahmanides is not the only one who shares the view that the Jewish people's experience in Egypt was a result of a sin Abraham committed. In the Talmud, Rabbi Eleazar reasoned that Egyptian servitude resulted from Abraham pressing scholars into military service during the voluntary war he waged in order to save Lot. Shmuel reasoned that he went too far in testing God's promise that he would inherit the land of Israel. Rabbi Yohanan asserted that it was because he returned the Sodomites to their king instead of proselytizing.[95] Each contention portrays the Egyptian servitude as punishment for a deficiency of faith. The miracles that God performed at the end of the Egyptian exile addressed each claim made that Abraham sinned through a lack of faith. God alone waged battle against the Egyptians, showing that one need not press Torah scholars into military service, with miracles never before seen, showing that one should not question God's word even if the result seems impossible, whereby even a mixed multitude left Egypt with the Jewish people, showing that one should not dismiss anyone due to an assumption that he cannot improve his ways. The idea of Egyptian servitude as a consequence of Abraham's sin considers Abraham as a nation, temporaneously of one, that is able to influence the tides of its future generations rather than solely as a precursor whose initiatives help ultimately shape a future nation. In

---

93 Nahmanides, Leviticus 15:12.
94 Nahmanides, Leviticus 12:10.
95 BT *Nedarim* 32a.

the Jewish tradition, this idea is conveyed by the expression that the actions of the forebears are a sign to their posterity.

The sages also consider the allusion to the four exiles in the prophecy of the covenant between the parts as a pledge to Abraham that God will protect the Jews in exile and redeem them when they have repented for their sins. Reinterpreting the topic of conversation between God and Abraham from his uncertainty that he will inherit the land to his consternation that his children will sin and be destroyed, the sages relay the following exchange:

> Abraham said, 'Master of the Universe, should Israel sin before You, will You do to them [as You did] to the generation of the Flood and to the generation of the Dispersion?' [God] replied to him, 'No.' He then said to Him, 'Master of the Universe, let me know whereby I shall inherit it.' [God] answered, 'Take Me a heifer of three years old, and a she-goat of three years old,' and so on. Abraham then continued, 'Master of the Universe! This holds good while the Temple remains in existence, but when the Temple no longer exists, what will become of them?' [God] replied, 'I have already long ago provided for them in the Torah the order of sacrifices. Whenever they read it, I will deem it as if they had offered them before Me and I will grant them pardon for all their iniquities.'[96]

This version of the conversation communicates that the covenant between the pieces is not a guarantee of exile but rather a guarantee that the Jews will survive the catharsis of exile and be redeemed untainted by sin. The sages transmit another discussion between God and Abraham which reinforces the idea that exile is an aberration and not a quotidian part of the history of the Jewish people. The midrash relates that God asked Abraham if he would prefer that his descendants pass through *Gehenom* or go into exile as atonement for sin. After vacillating between the two alternatives, Abraham chose exile, although there is disagreement as to whether

[96] BT *Ta'anit* 27b.

his choice was based on God's recommendation or on his own assessment.[97] The midrash clearly demonstrates that if exile is an inevitable part of Jewish history, it is not because it is necessary to fulfill Jewish universalism. Its association with *Gehenom* undoubtedly equates exile with punishment for sin. Furthermore, Abraham's indecision reveals his fear that exile could permanently erase the Jewish presence from the world whereas *Gehenom* is only a temporary condition in which the soul is purged after death. God's advice to choose exile does not imply that exile is an ideal condition in which the Jewish people may fulfill their universal goals. Instead, it offers Abraham confidence that despite the exile, the Jewish people will be able to withstand the threat of assimilation and fulfill its destiny at the time of redemption. While *Gehenom* expiates sin, it precludes the ideal fulfillment of Jewish destiny. Therefore, while exile is the better alternative, it is so only as an effective atonement for sin rather than the most desirable path towards fulfilling the Jewish people's historical goal.

In trying to find the proper balance for the authentic Jew living in contemporary times, one would do well to remember that Korah also used the idea that the Jewish people are a kingdom of priests and a holy nation to advocate a democratic Judaism. When he and his followers contested the legitimacy of Moses's juridical authority and Aharon's sacramental status, they said, "For everyone in the congregation is holy, every one of them, and Hashem is among them. Why then do you exalt yourselves above the assembly of Hashem?"[98] They essentially claimed that because everyone in the nation is holy, there is no need for a separate priestly caste to worship God properly, nor is a detached group of scholars needed to interpret God's law for the people. The halakhic queries that Korah puts to Moses illustrate this challenge. According to the midrash, Korah asked Moses the following: "A four-cornered

[97] *Genesis Rabbah* 44:21.
[98] Numbers 16:3.

garment requires fringes, one of which must be blue. Does a garment made entirely of blue wool require a blue fringe or not? Is it necessary to place a mezuzah on the doorpost of a room filled with Torah scrolls?" Both questions make the same conceptual comment. When the fabric of the community is the same and when all are equally in possession of the Torah, the singling out of a minority that appears to have no inherent uniqueness in order to sanctify the majority cannot be God's will but rather an arbitrary power play. The conclusion of the episode, in which the Israelites would have been destroyed but for the efforts of the very people who were distinguished, shows the self-destructive nature of a God-centered republic and substantiates the uniqueness of God's chosen leaders.

In claiming that the Jewish people were chosen by God for unknown reasons, that the land of Israel's significance is contingent upon Jewish sovereignty, and that the exile is a fundamental component of Jewish history, one may lose sight of the inherent, if not always apparent, uniqueness of the Jewish people and the land of Israel. This potential disregard may not only weaken the legitimacy of chosenness for insecure Jews, but it may easily lend itself to a perversion of the idea into racist nationalism in the eyes of the world. When one considers exile not as a consequence of sin but rather as a pedagogical tool, the holy congregation risks self-destruction and nullification into the greater cloth of life. Judaism, which is not a democratic system of theological equality, should not be made into one in order to win legitimacy from the nations. Chosenness is not to be understated or concealed. It should be considered with both dignity and the humility that it demands.

RABBI SOLOVEITCHIK: HALAKHA AS THE FOUNDATION OF A JEWISH *WELTANSCHAUUNG*

RABBI SOLOVEITCHIK ARGUES for the necessity of a wholly autonomous Jewish *Weltanschauung* whose epistemological foundation is derived solely from the cognitive data embedded within Halakha and whose existence is substantiated by intentional action. However, in transforming Halakha from a normative system into an ontological one, he does not fully explain how the intention of a religiously significant action reveals the existence of religious cognitive data or how rational intuition discovers the content upon which the ontological framework is developed.

For Rabbi Soloveitchik, the expression of religious thought, as opposed to the awareness of a religious experience, directly relates to the contemporaneous scientific-philosophical framework of the society in which the religious thinker lives. When science and philosophy share the same cognitive approach, the religious thinker will deliberately adopt, ignore, or reject their description of reality, creating a religious thought of either apologetics, agnosticism, or mysticism, but never can he develop a religious expression of the world without first considering the scientific-philosophical viewpoint. On the other hand, when the unity of interpretation shatters into a multiplicity of cognitive approaches, religious thought may offer an independent methodology for explaining reality.[1] In such an environment, religious thought does not claim to be the only legitimate way to understand the world. Instead, it

---

[1] *The Halakhic Mind*, 4.

asserts its authenticity alongside various other valid, even if contradicting, theories of reality. Religious thought can validate other philosophical methodologies because the idea of epistemological pluralism neither negates the singular nature of reality nor the veracity of conflicting approaches.

> Pluralism asserts only that the object reveals itself in manifold ways to the subject, and that a certain *telos* corresponds to each of these ontical manifestations. Subsequently, the philosopher or scientist may choose one of the many aspects of reality in compliance with his goal.[2]

The religious thinker may also choose to perceive the world as determined by a religious ontical manifestation. Although the reality in which he lives will be the same as that of the philosopher, it will demand a different manner of being given the different telos toward which he progresses.

While epistemological pluralism justifies the autonomy of religious thought, it does not explain how an autonomous religious epistemology develops. What in the religious experience lays the cognitive groundwork upon which the religious thinker can build his *Weltanschauung*?

> The noetic component of the religious experience must be independently examined. If and when an eidetic analysis discerns cognitive components in the religious act, then the theory of cognitive pluralism will substantiate the claim of religion to theoretical interpretation. However, as long as the cognitive component remains undiscovered, any attempt to justify religious knowledge is futile.[3]

Rabbi Soloveitchik argues that the cognitive component in the religious act lays in the intention of the religious actor. Because intention supposes predication, valuation, and only then the consummation of the act, the actor must have both religious

---

[2] *The Halakhic Mind*, 16.
[3] *The Halakhic Mind*, 41.

knowledge and the cognitive capabilities necessary for religious action.[4] In other words, in order to perform a religious deed, a person must first understand the world so as to manipulate it for the purpose of the deed and evaluate whether it is worth performing the deed. Only then will he perform it. It is not that intention itself is the cognitive data upon which religious thought is based. Rather, intention demonstrates that the intending actor possesses the requisite religious cognitive data to comprehend and evaluate his actions in light of a religious telos.

Religious cognitive material that constitutes the foundation of religious knowledge requires a religious schema to interpret and evaluate the material in relation to the telos of the religious ontical manifestation. This schema will represent concepts differently from another schema because the concept, or object, will be revealed differently. For example, while both the quantitative scientific conception and its qualitative humanistic counterpart consider time as a frame of reference for either physical existence or mental activity, the religious conception of time is as an independent entity with its own characteristics, such as holy or profane.[5] Because the religious schema is wholly independent of any scientific or philosophical approach to knowledge, its concepts cannot be understood except in the religious context. Therefore, while they are cognitive, religious ideas cannot be considered rational in the traditional sense of the term.

Rabbi Soloveitchik's proof of the existence of religious cognitive data, based upon the fact that when one intends to perform a religious act he must use cognitive data in order to establish his intention, seems to run a circular course. If one assumes that proof for the existence of religious cognitive data lies in the fact that a person performed a religious act intentionally, he must also assume that his intention was determined by a religious epistemology, which presupposes religious cognitive data upon

---

[4] *The Halakhic Mind*, 44.

[5] *The Halakhic Mind*, 47.

which it is based. If he does not assume that his intention was determined by a religious epistemology, he can no longer prove the existence of religious cognitive data from the intended action.

In addition, under Rabbi Soloveitchik's assumption, in order for an act to have religious significance it must be performed with a religious intention, for only with a religious intention could one understand his deed as a religious act in the context of the religious epistemology with which he sees the world. This idea corresponds to the concept that "the commandments require intention"[6] for one to properly fulfill them. As such, the physical act itself is not important per se; rather, its importance lies in its relation to the actor's intention, as it is only a consequence to the person's initial thought. Also, the reason for which one is acting would be more important than what causes him to act, since a cause can produce both intentional and unintentional, as well as voluntary and involuntary, actions, while a reason produces only intentional and voluntary actions.[7]

However, a single action may be perceived in several different contexts. For example, consider a person washing the dishes after eating dinner with his wife and another couple. The reason why he is washing the dishes may be to show his appreciation to his wife for having prepared the meal; because he prefers his kitchen to be clean; because he dislikes his guests' company and wants some private time doing mindless labor at the end of a hard day; or to offend his guests by being antisocial. If the person has only one of the above reasons for washing the dishes and does not know that he is showing his appreciation for his wife, offending his guests, or alleviating his anxiety over a dirty kitchen, then his only intended

[6] BT *Berakhot* 13a; *Hullin* 31a; *Eruvin* 96a; *Pesahim* 114b.

[7] See G.E.M. Anscombe, who writes: "[T]he more the action is described as a mere response, the more inclined one would be to the word 'cause;' while the more it is described as a response to something as having a significance that is dwelt on by the agent in his account, or as a response surrounded with thoughts and questions, the more inclined one would be to use the word 'reason.'" (*Intention,* 23–24)

action is *washing the dishes in order to escape conversation*; all other actions of washing dishes being unintended and thus outside his epistemological framework (at least until someone informs him of those consequences). To say that he washes the dishes *just* to wash the dishes may indicate an intentional action, yet the idea of intention in this example leaves the word without meaning for the purposes of building an epistemological framework.

Intention not only relates to the reason for someone's actions but also to the manner in which the action is performed. For example, the same man intends to wash the dishes, only this time the dishrag that he is using is filthy, since he used it earlier in the day to clean the tires on his car. Whether he remembers that the dishrag is filthy or not, he is intentionally using it on the dishes. One can no longer say that he is intentionally washing the dishes, because, on the contrary, they are getting dirtier. In this scenario, if washing dishes were a religious deed, the action should have religious significance. While it is not an intentional action, he did act with intention, though the consequences of his action were not what he desired. His action was, nevertheless, determined by a religious epistemology.

A question arises when the man intentionally performs the washing of the dishes and actually washes them, yet has two reasons for doing so. If one's reasons for washing the dishes were to keep a clean house and also to portray the absurdity of life since the dishes will only get dirty again at the next meal, in one action he has communicated two different, and possibly even contradictory, views of perceiving the world. The first intention demonstrates his belief in the importance of order and cleanliness in the proper maintenance of a household. The second intention portrays disdain at the socially constructed limits to life and the ineffectiveness that such limits have upon ultimate entropy. Even under Rabbi Soloveitchik's conception, where action is only considered a consequence of the mental intention, one could still not say that because the one action had two different intentions, he performed two different intentional actions. In performing this single intentional action, does he combine two ontological perspectives into one, whereby he sees the world with one confusing orientation? Or does he engage in perceiving the world in different ways simultaneously, each way having a different ontological framework yet sharing the same cognitive data that is interpreted according to the different schemata? In either case, if intention demonstrates the ability for cognitive data to be interpreted according to a religious epistemology, it should be important that the actor's intention have a religious interpretive component for the religious deed to be significant.

Judaism recognizes that while there are several types of actions that differ in terms of religious significance, each type can be classified under one of four major classes. A *happening* results from an unintended action that corresponds to the performance of a prescribed or prohibited action. An *intentional action (1)* corresponds to the performance of a prescribed or prohibited action, yet the actor only intends to perform the action and has no regard for its religious significance. In other words, he acts without a religious reason. An *intentional action (2)* corresponds to the performance of a prescribed or prohibited act, and the actor intends to perform the action and has regard for its religious significance. An *intentional action (3)* corresponds to the performance of a prescribed or prohibited action, yet the actor specifically does intend not to perform the action with regard for its religious significance.

We will first examine actions that take place outside a specifically religious context, such as during the Sabbath or holidays. If a knife were to fall on its own, happening to slaughter a cow in the ritually prescribed manner, the animal would not be rendered ritually fit. If, however, a person threw the knife, or it even fell from his hand, and it slaughtered a cow in the ritually prescribed manner, the animal would be considered ritually fit.[8] If a person intentionally slaughtered the animal with a specifically anti-religious intent, such as for idolatry, the animal would not be ritually

[8] *Shulhan Arukh, Yoreh Deah* 3:1.

fit for consumption.[9] The falling of the knife is considered a non-action, since no person was an actor in this event. On the other hand, every class of actions mentioned has religious significance with regard to ritual slaughter. Throwing the knife is a *happening*, since the slaughtering was not an intended act, yet still the animal is ritually fit for consumption. *Intentional action (1)*, and obviously *intentional action (2)*, renders the animal fit. Although *intentional action (3)* has religious effect, it adds nothing new to the analysis, since if the person has the distinct intention to not fulfill a commandment then he obviously has a religious epistemology in which he understands the value of religiously prescribed or prohibited actions. This example demonstrates that even if a person has no religious intent whatsoever, his action still has religious significance.

A similar example is found in the realm of ritual purity. If a woman, after completing her prescribed time of separation, fell accidentally into a body of water that could be used as an immersion pool, or immersed in such a body of water only in order to cool herself, she would be permitted to her husband as if she had intentionally immersed for that purpose.[10] While some consider falling into the water as having no religious significance, they are willing to confer such significance upon an event in which someone else pushes her into the water in order for her to fulfill the prescribed immersion.[11] In the case of both ritual slaughter and immersion, regardless of which opinion one follows, the requirement for religious intention in order for the action to have religious significance is minimal. The woman's feeling the sensation of the water enveloping her, whether she fell into it or was pushed, is a *happening*, yet it still confers ritual purity. It certainly does not necessitate a religious epistemology.[12]

---

[9] *Shulhan Arukh*, *Yoreh Deah* 4:1.

[10] *Hilkhot Mikva'ot* 1:8; *Shulhan Arukh*, *Yoreh Deah* 198:48.

[11] Rema, *Yoreh Deah* 198:48.

[12] There is a difference in the action of falling into the water and being pushed, yet the difference further confirms the lack of necessity of intent for an action to be religiously significant. According to the idea that the woman must be pushed, the

Requisite religious intention differs, however, for actions that have psychological, rather than purely physical, effects.[13] For example, in order for the recital of the *Shema*, *kiddush*, the blessing after meals, or prayer to have religious significance, a person must intend both to state the required words and intend that the recital fulfill its psychological purpose.[14] Psychologically influencing actions cannot be used to prove the existence of a religious epistemology developed from the cognitive material of the intended action because the action itself is supposed to reinforce the religious ontological framework. To recite the *Shema* or to pray without understanding the meaning of the words cannot be considered an intentional act,[15] unless he recites the words because he likes the sound it makes. If the latter is the reason, however, there is no value to the words being said; they are gibberish. To prove the ability to form a religious epistemology from the cognitive data that one uses in intending to perform a psychologically influencing action would be putting the cart before the horse, since it is obvious, by virtue of comprehending his voluntary statements that he has a certain religious worldview.

When a person performs an action in a sanctified context, meaning either on the Sabbath or on a holiday, the role that

---

woman falling into a mikveh would be compared to a knife falling and ritually slaughtering an animal. In both cases, there is no human force as a cause of the action. On the other hand, the woman who is pushed, like the knife that is thrown, is involved in an action with a human, as opposed to natural, cause. The focus of the debate, when seen in this light, is not about whether intention makes an act religiously significant but rather if human causation is necessary or if human awareness is enough to consider something a religiously significant action, even if it is only a *happening*.

13 Although one can argue that the impurity resulting from a woman's menstrual cycle is spiritual rather than physical, my meaning is that the spiritual state has physical consequences, such as the necessity of refraining from physical intimacy until the physical act of immersion.

14 *Mishna Berurah,* Chapter 60, s.v. "Some say." Leniency regarding how much of the recital requires both types of intention is only due to the recognition of the difficulty for most people to concentrate for long periods of time.

15 *Be'er Heitiv*, *Orah Hayyim* 62:2.

intention plays in determining the act's religious significance is still the same, though with a slightly greater requirement. For example, if a person intentionally removes a vegetable from the ground on the Sabbath, yet does not know that his act is prohibited or that it is the Sabbath, his action has religious significance, but of a lesser severity than if he intended the action with knowledge of the context in which the action took place.[16] If he intends a certain action yet performs a different one, for example he intended to pick up cut vegetables but the vegetables he thought had been cut were actually still in the ground, from which he removed them inadvertently, or he intended to remove the pepper on the right from the ground but instead removed the cucumber on the left, his actions would not be religiously significant.[17] From these examples, it seems as if the intent to complete the action, in and of itself, is the determining factor, rather than understanding the context in which one is acting. If a person acts as he intended, it does not matter whether he recognized his existential position. His actions still have consequences. On the other hand, if the intended act is unsuccessful, his knowledge of the religious context of his intended action is not enough to have a religious effect.[18]

---

[16] He is considered as a person who sinned unknowingly and must bring a sin-offering to the Temple.

[17] These examples are considered to be within the category of *mit'asek,* which does not create a liability.

[18] Even though we have determined that intentionality of action determines religious significance, we must address why awareness of the intentional action's context also has religious implication, i.e. in determining the form of punishment. One could postulate that the reason for the importance of awareness with regards to the Sabbath, when context would not have such influence for a mundane environment, is not due to the sanctity of the day per se, but rather in how we are commanded regarding it. The commandments of the Sabbath are given under "Protect the Sabbath day," and "Remember the Sabbath day." We consider the prohibition to perform intentional actions of a creative nature under the rubric of "Protect the Sabbath day" while "Remember the Sabbath day" is typical held to support sanctifying the day with kiddush and havdala. One must be aware, however, that the two performances of sanctification at the beginning and end of the day are supposed to instill in one's consciousness the sanctification of the Sabbath, i.e. we are commanded to be aware of the context of the day. Therefore,

This conclusion applies to other areas of sanctified time as well. For example, if one intentionally eats unleavened bread solely for the sake of eating it, without any religious motivation, or is forced to eat it even by non-Jews (an even greater leniency than in the case of immersion) – if he knows that it is the first night of Passover and therefore he is required to eat it, his act has religious significance. If he intended to eat leavened bread on the first night but instead ate unleavened bread, or he intentionally ate unleavened bread thinking that it was not Passover, his action has no religious significance, since both are failed intentional actions of eating a particular substance at a particular time.[19] Here, too, a *happening* and an *intentional action (1)* have religious significance. The reason why the failed intentional action has no religious significance in the context of Passover but has such significance in the context of the Sabbath is because during Passover the event consists of a positive fulfillment of a religious act, while during the Sabbath the event yields a negative consequence for a religious transgression. The negative consequence obligated by the failed intentional action is either punishment or expiation for being negligent of one's contextual awareness,[20] which in the realm of prescription parallels the negative consequence of not fulfilling a commandment.[21]

---

the intentional action from which we are proscribed is of a double nature, it is not just to intend upon the act but to intend upon the act with awareness of its context. Nevertheless, because an intentional action is committed even when awareness of the day is not present, such action must also be punished, albeit less stringently.

19 *Shulhan Arukh*, *Orah Hayyim* 475:4.

20 See *Sha'ar ha-Gemul* by Nahmanides.

21 The parallel between the Sabbath and Passover with regards to necessity of awareness of context is demonstrated by the fact of the commandment to discuss the Exodus of Egypt, which is incumbent upon everyone during the time of eating unleavened bread (see *Mekhilta d'Rabbi Ishmael,* Bo, Parsha 17). The ideal performance of the commandment would be the intentional action of eating unleavened bread with the awareness that it is Passover; however, in the case where he eats for enjoyment (or is force fed) but knows the context of the day there still would be an action which has religious significance, albeit of a lesser degree but still fulfilling the obligation. Where he intended to eat leavened but ate unleavened bread or intentionally ate unleavened bread but thought it was not

Intentional action in a sanctified context requires a higher standard of cognitive volition than in an ordinary context since the context itself demands a level of awareness of its sanctity. To act intentionally in such a situation, one must be aware of the sanctity of the day as part of the world in which he lives. Once he understands his current world, the degree of intention necessary corresponds to that of everyday life. Similarly, actions that are primarily of psychological import, such as hearing the shofar on Rosh ha-Shana, bear the same relationship between ordinary and sanctified contexts as physical actions, by requiring a higher level of intention within the higher standard of the sanctified context just like for the recital of the *Shema*, which requires a higher standard within the ordinary context.[22]

From the above examples, it seems that Rabbi Soloveitchik's contention that one can recognize the existence of religious cognitive data from the intention behind a religiously significant action may not be the case. An act may be religiously significant whether the one who performed it intended it to be so or not. His lack of awareness of its religious significance does not negate it. Instead, it negates the ability to claim definitively that the actor has a religious epistemology – which, in turn, raises doubt concerning the necessity of an autonomous ontological framework to achieve a religious telos. Like the person who washes the dishes for more than one reason, one may perceive a religiously significant action within a single yet multi-faceted framework whereby he can, for example, give money to the poor in such a way that he fulfills his religious obligation to give charity and also receives the desired honor of reading from the Torah on the Sabbath for all to see.[23]

Even if one cannot determine the existence of religious cognitive material from the intentions of a religiously significant

---

Passover, he either did not perform a religiously significant intentional action or his intentional action could not be said to have the full intent necessary, due to the obligation of awareness, for it to be religiously significant.

[22] *Shulhan Arukh*, *Orah Hayyim* 589:8.

[23] Taz, *Yoreh Deah* 249:1.

action, this does not negate the possibility of its existence nor the existence of a religious epistemology that is based upon it. There exist two potential methodologies, phenomenology and logicism, upon which a religious schema might be based. Rabbi Soloveitchik interjects his own moral sentiment in preferring logicism over phenomenology as the structure for a religious ontology. Claiming that the validity of any ontological perspective must be measured with consideration to its ethical implications, he argues that because phenomenological philosophies have been proven to lead to moral corruption, religious thought should avoid anything but the strictest adherence to an analytical methodology for fear of justified moral depravity in the religious sphere.

> The individual who frees himself from the rational principle and who casts off the yoke of objective thought will in the end turn destructive and lay waste the entire created order. Therefore, it is preferable that religion should ally itself with the forces of clear, logical cognition, as uniquely exemplified in the scientific method, even though at times the two might clash with one another, rather than pledge its troth to beclouded, mysterious ideologies that grope in the dark corners of existence, unaided by the shining light of objective knowledge, and believe that they have penetrated to the secret core of the world.[24]

Because religion claims its legitimacy as deriving from divine authority, it must not be defined in subjective phenomenological terms but rather by universal, objective principles.

By subjecting varying philosophical schools of thought to moral scrutiny, Rabbi Soloveitchik greatly undermines epistemological pluralism by validating only those that resemble science in their methodologies. His elimination of alternatives to the scientific method has one of two possible consequences. He either reunites science and philosophy, negating his previous justification for autonomous religious thought, or he replaces philosophy with

---

[24] *Halakhic Man*, 141.

religion as the alternative to the scientific world-view, in which both share the same method of comprehension and differ only in expression of content. Rabbi Soloveitchik admits to conflating science and philosophy by claiming that all philosophy that is independent of scientific methodology is arbitrary and unsound, yet he still leaves room for autonomous religious thought. Religion's independence from science stems from the differing objective constructs of each, which serve as the cognitive material for their respective schema.

Where the foundation of objective rationalism, and all subsequent scientific enquiry, is mathematics, autonomous Jewish thought develops from Halakha. Using Halakha as the analytic philosopher would use mathematics – i.e., to create an a priori ideal framework which he can compare to and thus understand reality – Halakha is no longer a normative code of living but a system of epistemological and ontological principles.[25] Rather than describing reality, Halakha imposes order onto reality so that the darkness of phenomenological existence can be brought to a cognitive light.

Both the mathematician and the halakhist gaze at the concrete world from an a priori, ideal standpoint, using a priori categories and concepts that determine from the outset their relationship to the qualitative phenomena they encounter. As both examine empirical reality from the vantage point of an ideal reality, they equally raise the question: Does this real phenomenon correspond to my ideal construction?[26]

Because Halakha parallels existence, every particular aspect of reality has a halakhic counterpart, and even more significant, every particular in Halakha is of absolute existential importance.[27] If the two do not correlate exactly, the halakhist, like the mathematician, does not alter his ideal model to fit reality. The abstract law

---

[25] "J.B. Soloveitchik's Philosophy of Halakha," 148.
[26] *Halakhic Man*, 23.
[27] *Be-Sod ha-Yahid ve-ha-Yahad*, 232.

maintains its position, while reality is considered anomalous and in a state of temporary aberration.[28]

Even the manner in which the halakhist determines his cognitive paradigm reflects the theorizing of the mathematician. While Rabbi Soloveitchik maintains the eternality of Halakha to the degree of asserting that it cannot be changed or revised,[29] "Halakhic man received the Torah from Sinai not as a simple recipient but as a creator of worlds, as a partner with the Almighty in the act of creation. The power of creative interpretation is the very foundation of the received tradition."[30] The analogy between the halakhist and the mathematician at this point becomes a bit stretched for one must now respond to the fact that the halakhist is given what the mathematician must discover on his own. Discovering the mathematical principles that one then interprets in order to objectify reality reflects greater cognitive creativity, for the ideal architecture upon which he has built his ideal world seemingly comes from naught. Interpreting received halakhic principles in a new way is an innovation, but renovating a house cannot compare with its initial construction. Rabbi Soloveitchik dismisses this incongruity by comparing the halakhist to the *modern* mathematician whose creativity is bound within the confines of the mathematical postulates of those who preceded him. In this way, neither the halakhist nor the mathematician discovers anything *ex nihilo*. Rather, each is improving upon the understanding of revealed concepts in innovative ways.

Any innovative idea that the halakhist, and by extension the mathematician, may propose is subject to the absolute authority of logic. No matter how eloquent or accurate the idea may seem to be, if it is not logically consistent with the cognitive framework in which it is meant to be understood, there is no place for it and it is rejected as false. The manner in which the halakhist discovers a new

---

28 *Halakhic Man*, 28.
29 "*U-Vikashtem mi-Sham*," 49.
30 *Halakhic Man*, 81.

halakhic paradigm, on the other hand, speaks less of pure logical deduction and more towards an unearthing by the intimate theorist who had sought it out. The halakhist not only depends on intuitive revelation to discover innovative interpretations; he also relies on intuition when resolving a doubt in objective halakhic principles.

> This intuition of the [halakhic] tradition is the source of halakhic decision and creative innovation. The meticulous intellect is not the founder of the accurate [halakhic] definition or the clear [halakhic] formulation but rather it [only] ponders what the perceiving soul provides him. Halakhic man, who is married to the Torah and cleaves to it, 'sees' the halakhic gists, 'feels' the halakhic ideas as if they were concrete sounds, visions, or fragrances. He lives not only in Halakha, but also with Halakha parallel to the way he lives in the world and with the world of color, melody, fragrance, and temperature. At this stage the Torah is revealed to man not only on the level of understanding, indicating a tranquil, clear, and controlled cognition but rather it also comes via the conduit of the realm of wisdom which from it flows rational intuition, the creator of the illustrative and deep vision and which conquers the desert of existence. The man who is married to the Torah opens [his process of comprehension] of the Torah with the heart and seals [his comprehension] of the Torah with the brain. The creative halakhic action begins not in rational analysis but rather in a vision, not in the [rational] formulation but rather in [intellectual] restlessness, not in light of elucidated logic but rather in the darkness which precedes logic.[31]

Under this conception, the rules of halakhic derivation and mathematical proof only confirm what the halakhist and the mathematician already knew by intuition.

Elsewhere, Rabbi Soloveitchik discusses the nature of halakhic intuition, whereby he differentiates between the interpretation and creative innovation of the mathematician and of the halakhist.

---

[31] *Be-Sod ha-Yahid ve-ha-Yahad*, 219.

Although both mathematics and Halakha create ontological systems, Halakha, unlike mathematics, cannot be divorced from the axiological premises held by the halakhist. He explains,

> Since the halakhic gesture is not to be abstracted from the person engaged in it, I cannot see how it is possible to divorce halakhic cognition from axiological premises or from an ethical motif. If halakhic research were limited to its interpretive phase – deciphering some obscure texts – such a discrepancy between the logical and the axiological judgments would be warranted. Since, however, halakhic thought is creative, original, flowing from the inner recesses and mysterious spring-wells of the personality where logical-cognitive and ethico-axiological motives are interwoven, any attempt at separation would result in crippling human creativity. From my own experience I know that in any halakhic investigation I have always been guided by a dim intuitive feeling which pointed out to me the true path, and this intuition has never been stripped of an ethical intention.[32]

Rabbi Soloveitchik's contention that if the halakhic gesture cannot be abstracted from the person, then halakhic cognition cannot be divorced from an ethical motif begs for further elucidation. If the ethico-axiological motives are themselves halakhic principles, then there should be no reason to assume abstraction is necessary, since the halakhist is not favoring any position over another but rather is only logically deriving a correct decision from its proper ontological premises. The fact that those ontological premises have normative content should be as relevant in the cognitive process as the law of gravity having physical consequences. If, however, the dim intuitive feeling has an ethical intention outside the realm of an halakhic ontology, then Halakha can no longer be seen as an a priori system that encompasses all of reality unless we are resigned to argue that

[32] *Community, Covenant and Commitment*, 276.

the influence of the ethical is anomalous and should be considered a temporary aberration. Putting the understanding of how the ethical motif influences the nature of halakhic intuition aside, it is important to understand the process of intuition itself as it relates to Halakha and mathematics.

Philosophers of mathematics are divided into two groups, each propounding one of two different conceptual understandings of the nature of mathematical intuition. According to the first group, intuition is a conceptualization of abstractions of sensory or imaginatory objects which are then manipulated according to internalized mathematical principles. In this sense, intuition is only an abstract form of rationality; it is ordinary perception or imagination conceptualized in a novel way.[33] In support of the idea that intuition is not an independent perception of the abstract, but rather an abstract perception of the real, George Berry writes:

> How then do we find out about this realm of extramental, nonparticular, unobservable entities? Our knowledge of them, like our knowledge of the extramental, unobservable objects of the physical sciences, is indirect, being tied to perceived things by a fragile web of theory. In both cases – physics and logic – our hypotheses about the unperceived are tested by their success in accounting for the character of the perceived. Misreading this similarity, one might easily conclude that a faculty of non-sensory perception, call it 'intuition,' is necessary to play a part in logic parallel to the role of sensation in physics. The conclusion is groundless. Long-run success in dealing with the same old perceptual field of ordinary sensation holistically confirms not only our belief in a force satisfying an inverse-square law but also, if more remotely, our belief in the derivatives used to compute the force. It also confirms our belief in the classes

33 "Mathematical Intuition," 211.

> ultimately invoked to so analyze the derivatives as to explain the computations.[34]

A mathematical example for the notion that mathematical intuition is an abstraction from ordinary perception would be the proof for the infinitude of prime numbers. We currently prove this theorem through the use of abstract logic and not just by imagining another prime number greater than the one we previously thought. Euclid, who first proved the infinitude of prime numbers, also gave a logical proof, yet it is obvious from the manner in which he writes that the idea stemmed from conceptualizing the real world and not solely perceiving the ideal one in which he was working.[35] Lord Byron gives a similar account of this type of intuition in the realm of physics: "When Newton saw an apple fall, he found/In that slight startle from his contemplation –/'Tis said (for I'll not answer above ground/For any sage's creed or calculation) –/A mode of proving that the earth turn'd round/In a most natural whirl, called 'gravitation;'/And this is the sole mortal who could grapple,/Since Adam, with a fall or with an apple."[36] A possible halakhic analogy could be seen in the incident between Hillel and the Benei Beteira. Once, when the fourteenth of Nisan fell on the Sabbath, the Benei Beteira forgot whether the Passover offering was to be sacrificed or not. They summoned Hillel, who supported his intuitive response with various halakhic arguments in defense of sacrificing the

---

[34] "Logic with Platonism," 261.

[35] See Euclid's *Elements,* Book 9, Proposition 20, where his proof stems from the visualization of line lengths to show that the actual number of prime numbers is more than any assigned multitude of prime numbers. Euclid's notion of infinity was drawn from a conception that something finite, like a line, could be extended indefinitely. The modern notion, on the other hand, would conceptualize an infinite line with the admission that one can only perceive a part of it. For this reason Euclid did not write that there are infinitely many prime numbers, but rather that the prime numbers are more than any assigned multitude of prime numbers.

[36] *Don Juan,* Canto 10.

Passover offering on the Sabbath. All of his rational justifications were refuted by the scholarly elite. His halakhic decision was only finally accepted when he confessed that his ruling, although supported by rational arguments, came to him from the mouths of his teachers, Shemaya and Avtalyon. The scholarly elite then asked Hillel, "Master, what if a man forgot and did not bring a knife on the eve of the Sabbath?" Hillel admitted that he had forgotten the ruling, yet he stated, "But leave it to Israel. If they are not prophets, yet they are the sons of prophets." The following day, they saw that a man whose Passover offering was a lamb had stuck the knife in its wool and a man whose Passover offering was a goat stuck the knife between its horns. After seeing the way the people behaved, he remembered the Halakha and said, "Thus have I received the tradition from the mouths of Shemaya and Avtalyon."[37] Hillel's halakhic intuition could not be justified solely by the rules of halakhic derivation; only the admission of physically hearing the Halakha from his teachers and perceiving how a finite number of people acted in reality allowed the ideal conception of Halakha to be accepted.

Rabbi Soloveitchik rejects this constructivist theory of intuition for two reasons. The first reason is based on his view of Halakha in general. Because theoretical Halakha is an ideal system without any definitional relationship to the physical world, the physical world cannot determine what the ideal Halakha should be. Abstraction from physical halakhic acts may give us a conceptual commonality that could be used to theorize about the nature of future cases; however, if the physical world temporarily aberrates from the halakhic ideal, any abstraction from the physical world is irrelevant. The second reason why Rabbi Soloveitchik rejects a constructivist theory of intuition is to prevent any possibility for Halakha to be

---

[37] Tosefta *Pesahim* 4:11; JT *Pesahim* 39a; BT *Pesahim* 66a.

used to justify moral depravity. Commenting on such a phenomenon in secular philosophy, he writes,

> It is no mere coincidence that the most celebrated philosophers of the third Reich were outstanding disciples of Husserl. Husserl's intuitionism (*Wesensschau*) which Husserl, a trained mathematician, strove to keep on the level of mathematical intuition, was transposed into emotional approaches to reality. When reason surrenders its supremacy to dark, equivocal emotions, no dam is able to stem the tide of the affective stream.[38]

The ease with which one can find justification for his immoral desires after the fact, by idealizing the actions of the immoral majority and castigating the ethical minority as an aberration, is too strong to allow a religious worldview, whose principles carry the weight of God's authority, to be conceived by its methodology.

The second conceptual understanding of mathematical intuition, which Rabbi Soloveitchik applies to halakhic intuition as well, is associated with mathematical Platonism. According to mathematical Platonism, mathematical concepts actually exist, yet in the realm of the ideal and not as part of physical reality. Because they are not part of our physical reality, however, a person cannot perceive them in the manner in which they can perceive a physical object; the five senses for the physical world are impotent in the realm of the ideal.[39] As Kurt Gödel has popularly stated,

> But, despite their remoteness from sense experience, we do have something like a perception also of the objects of set theory, as is seen from the fact that the axioms force themselves upon us as being true. I don't see any reason why we should have less confidence in this kind of

---

[38] *The Halakhic Mind*, 53.

[39] Intuition cannot be considered as unconscious inference because inferential knowledge, whether unconscious or conscious, is based on knowledge already perceived, leaving the manner of discernment of ideal concepts still in doubt.

> perception, i.e., in mathematical intuition, than in sense perception.[40]

If mathematical intuition is equivalent to sense perception, the moral difficulty that Rabbi Soloveitchik has with the first conception of intuition arises here as well. Because there is no way to test one's intuition except via rational proof – the concept is not bound by its encounter with the physical world – there is no way to refute one's conviction except by another's retort. In the event that others disagree, rational argument will seldom convince one who holds his truth to be self-evident, for the ease of justifying what one already thinks is right is much greater than what he wants to be right. Intuition becomes the catchall defense for any philosophical or religious conviction. As Gottlob Frege remarks, "We are all too ready to invoke inner intuition, whenever we cannot produce any other ground of knowledge."[41] For Rabbi Soloveitchik to maintain his requirement of absolute objectivity in the development of a religious worldview, he must consider the innate subjectivity of Platonistic intuition and the constraints that rational analysis will have in limiting the strength of intuition when it is held to the veridical level of sensory perception.

The comparison of a Platonic view of mathematics to Halakha has another difficult consequence to accept for a religious ontological framework. By turning normative Halakha into epistemological and ontological principles, Rabbi Soloveitchik seems to sacrifice the concept of free will. To illustrate, $1 + 1 = 2$ is a tautology, there can never be a case where this mathematical statement is not true. Similarly, every particle in the Universe attracts every other with a force which is proportional to the products of their masses and inversely proportional to the square of

---

[40] *Philosophy of Mathematics*, 483–484.
[41] *The Foundations of Arithmetic*, 19.

their separation;[42] there can never be a case where this statement of the laws of physics is not true. These statements are part of the ideal world which is a cognitive analogy to the physical world. Is man bound by the ideal world of Halakha in the same way? According to Rabbi Soloveitchik, he is.

> [H]alakhic man does not experience any consciousness of compulsion accompanying the norm. Rather, it seems to him as though he discovered the norm in his innermost self, as though it was not just a commandment that had been imposed upon him, but an existential law of his very being.[43]

The halakhic man has no evil inclination. His recognition of the laws of halakhic nature allows him to live his life accordingly without any sense of choice, for just as one cannot choose to defy the laws of gravity, so too Halakha.

Attributing to Halakha the same causality as the laws of mathematics or physics not only contradicts the Talmudic dictum, "The greater the man, the greater his evil inclination,"[44] but it also does not account for the existence of sin in the world. If Halakha is as Rabbi Soloveitchik describes, then just because someone is not a halakhic man does not mean that he is able to transgress Halakha. That would be equivalent to saying that one has the ability to defy gravity as long as he is not aware of its laws! To say that sin is a result of a temporary aberration in the physical world from the ideal world of Halakha still does not allow for the possibility of free will, since any physical aberration would be a systemic, involuntary disjunction between the abstract principle and actual events, not the particular consequence of a deliberate choice.

While it is true that internalizing the spirit of Halakha will allow one to use Halakha as a basis for a Jewish perspective on life, it is

---

42 Newton's Law of Universal Gravitation (taken within the context of Einstein's Theory of General Relativity).
43 *Halakhic Man*, 65.
44 BT *Sukkah* 52a.

difficult to agree with Rabbi Soloveitchik that it is the only source from which a Jewish *Weltanschauung* could emerge.[45] To claim that Halakha is an ideal conceptual framework independent of reality and still maintain that it could give understanding to the reality of which it has no relation is either contradictory or a paradox which is beyond my humble grasp. Halakha necessarily will shape the way people think by virtue of its pedagogical character; nevertheless, a Jewish *Weltanschauung* consists of more than just a normative system. The Torah encompasses history, poetry, mysticism, literature, philosophy, and many other facets of reality, as well as Halakha. A Jewish world view should do the same.

45 *The Halakhic Mind*, 101.

Rabbi Berkovits: Halakha as Divine Ethics

In creating a secular ethics based solely upon reason, modern man has reached the conclusion that religion is no longer essential as a system of governing behavior and that divine laws ought to be replaced with universal maxims. Rabbi Berkovits endeavors to salvage religion from the depths of irrelevancy by demonstrating that rationality has neither the authority to obligate man to act nor the power to compel man to perform according to what reason deduces as the proper moral action. According to him, only divine religion possesses the required authority and its laws the necessary physical inducement to make man moral. By transforming religion into a divine system of ethics, however, Rabbi Berkovits establishes a tenuous justification for religion and resigns divine law to the dictates of man's reason.

Rabbi Berkovits claims that the argument for the efficacy of secular ethics in causing man to become moral begins in Greek philosophy. If, through rational investigation, one is able to discover which actions will engender him to develop the virtues which assist in attaining *eudaimonia*, he will certainly act accordingly to reach his ultimate goal. Reason, therefore, both can obligate and compel man to behave with a focus towards his own moral refinement, leaving the necessity of religion unfounded. The acceptance of the capability of reason at the expense of reliance on revelation in determining moral conduct can be seen in the medieval debates on whether the ideal of the good exists independently or solely by virtue of God's will. Rabbi Saadia Gaon offers a compromise position that affirms the competency of reason while maintaining the necessity of revelation. To the question of revelation's purpose in the face of reason, he answers,

> We say, then, [that] the All-Wise knew that the conclusions reached by means of the art of speculation could be attained only in the course of a certain measure of time. If, therefore, He had referred us for our acquaintance with His religion to that art alone, we would have remained without religious guidance whatever for a while, until the process of reasoning was completed by us so that we could make use of its conclusions. But many a one of us might never complete the process because of some flaw in his reasoning.[1]

This justification, however, opens the door for later thinkers to argue that revelation is only a matter of expediency and not of necessity, which allows for the eventual claim that religion is altogether superfluous. Rabbi Saadia does recognize that there is a differentiation between rational, moral commandments and ritual commandments, which, he claims, have no moral worth per se but are commanded to bestow reward for their adherence, yet due to his veneration of reason he is unable to completely abandon a rational justification for even the ritual commandments.[2]

During the Enlightenment, arguing for revelation as a necessary foundation for ethics became futile. Reason triumphed and became the source of both ethics and religion, and man replaced the divine as the moral authority. To quote Immanuel Kant, the protagonist of the modern axiological debate:

> Morality, then, is the relation of actions to the autonomy of the will, that is, to the potential universal legislation by its maxims. An action that is consistent with the autonomy of the will is permitted; one that does not agree therewith is forbidden. A will whose maxims necessarily coincide with the laws of autonomy is a holy will, good absolutely. The

[1] *Beliefs and Opinions*, 31.
[2] *Beliefs and Opinions*, 141.

> dependence of a will not absolutely good on the principle (moral necessitation) is obligation. This, then, cannot be applied to a holy being. The objective necessity of actions from obligation is called duty.[3]

Under Kant's philosophy, revelation came from God but arose from man. Universal law, determined by one's own reason, impels the will to act according to its dictates. The holy man is the autonomous person whose will does not conflict with his higher ideals, and the man who is not holy is bound by the law he imposes upon himself. For Kant, God serves a purpose only in attributing legality to the public ordinances of an ethical community, since ethical actions are private by nature. The ordinances themselves, however, originate from the ethos of the ethical community itself, further diminishing God's role in man's religion of reason.[4]

Rabbi Berkovits first endeavors to restore God and divine revelation as a necessity for moral development by denying that reason has any ethical authority. Man's free will allows for the choice to behave unethically; simply knowing right and wrong does not obligate a person to act accordingly.[5] He writes, "Reason may tell the difference between right and wrong; perhaps even the difference between good and evil. It cannot, however, provide the obligation for doing good and eschewing evil. The source of all obligation is a will, and the motivation of a will is a desire."[6] Because a rational act results from the will choosing to follow the dictates of reason, the will is the true authority of action. However, since man's will is fickle and allows him to succumb to temptation, absolute ethical authority can only originate in the revelation of the divine will. Law in and of itself, whether it be moral or religious, is insignificant without the authority imposed upon it by the lawgiver. Therefore, it is wrong to claim the possibility of a religion within

---

[3] *Fundamental Principles of the Metaphysics of Morals*, 71.
[4] *Religion within the Boundaries of Mere Reason*, 110.
[5] *God, Man and History*, 95.
[6] *God, Man and History*, 103.

the boundaries of reason alone since the rationality of the law in no way contradicts the necessity of a divine origin. Rational law may be eternal truth, but only the will of God transforms the ethical act into an absolute religious imperative.

While religion alone creates an absolute ethical obligation, Rabbi Berkovits allows for the existence of secular ethics. Both systems of social behavior may even consist of exactly the same parameters, only differing in the origins of their respective obligating authorities. This difference, however, separates true morality from social etiquette. To quote Rabbi Berkovits,

> But a law instituted by a will of relative authority admits of compromise for the sake of expediency; the law of absolute authority will not be overruled by such considerations. All secular ethics lack the quality of absolute obligation. They are as changeable as the desires and the wills that institute them; the law of God alone is as eternal as His will.[7]

Religion thus is proved to be the only true ethical guide, combining rationality with an authority that is absolute.[8] In creating a system whereby religion and ethics only differ in the nature of moral obligation, Rabbi Berkovits has succeeded Rabbi Saadia Gaon in finding a new compromise which affirms reason yet necessitates revelation.

The foundation for Rabbi Berkovits's denial of rational authority stems from man's free will to choose whether to act as reason would dictate or not. However, man's ability to choose to obey or reject authority in a particular instance does not devalue the essence of the authority in general. Obligation is compulsion upon someone to act in a certain way whether he wishes to do so or not. Authority entails the legitimacy to impose the obligation. Contrary to Rabbi Berkovits's claim that Kant only demonstrated that the categorical imperative is a requirement for rational action but failed to show why it is imperative, Kant recognized that it is the will that

---

[7] *God, Man and History*, 106.
[8] *God, Man and History*, 106.

compels action. However, reason is the authority that obligates the will to compel action to be in line with its standards. Because he believed that the will does not have authority, Kant said,

> A perfectly good will would therefore be equally subject to objective laws (viz., laws of good), but could not be conceived as obliged thereby to act lawfully, because of itself from its subjective constitution it can only be determined by the conception of good.... Therefore imperatives are only formulae to express the relation of objective laws of all volition to the subjective imperfection of the will of this or that rational being, for example, the human will.[9]

If Rabbi Berkovits is to critique Kant, it should not be that he failed to understand the source of obligation. Rather, it should be that by defining the will as practical reason and by claiming that the categorical imperative is a consequence of pure practical reason, his theory of moral obligation becomes so abstract that it has little relevance for directing ethical conduct in everyday life.

In defining the will as the source of obligation and desire its motivation, Rabbi Berkovits explains how a person could willingly act counter to what would be perceived as the rational decision. Willing deflection from reason demonstrates that the will has greater influence than rationality on man's conduct and is therefore the true source of obligation. Reason is only a guide for the will and only advises on the most effective process to carry out what man has already willed to do. If we accept the assumption that the will, distinct from reason, is the real authority, what is the essence of the will that it possesses such authority, and how does desire play a role in its motivation? If any desire can motivate the will indiscriminately to authorize its implementation, any base act is justified in that it is the fulfillment of an authorized obligation. This conception of the will negates rather than upholds the idea of ethics and leaves man no better than animals. King Solomon says of the moral worth of

---

[9] *Fundamental Principles of the Metaphysics of Morals*, 31.

those who live for the fulfillment of their own pleasure, "Then I said in my heart concerning the sons of man: God has selected them out, but only to see that in themselves they are as beasts. For the fate of the sons of man and the fate of the beast – theirs is one fate. As one dies so dies the other, and all have the same spirit. So the superiority of man over beast is naught for all is vanity."[10] Rabbi Berkovits must assume that there is a prioritization of desire, that man separates desires into those that are acted upon in order to receive immediate gratification and those that entail reflective self-evaluation. In this hierarchical structure, the will is motivated by the desire to be rather than by the desire to do.

A desire stemming from reflective self-evaluation, however, only arises when one rationally understands what constitutes a desirable means of being. The recognition that a particular way of being is desirable, together with the motivation of the will to authorize those actions that characterize that particular mode of being, demonstrates the influence of reason upon the authority of the will. Rabbi Berkovits may be correct in stating that reason can only obligate a person if he desires the actualization of that which is reasonable. However, he must admit that one will only desire the actualization of that which is reasonable if he thinks that it is something he ought to desire. In a situation where someone acts voluntarily in a manner that is contrary to the perceived rational action, he may have neither rejected the authority of reason nor acted according to his will. His actions may be the result of temptations that have overpowered his will in a moment of weakness. One particular example in which Halakha recognizes the possibility that a conflict among desires may result in action against one's own will is the fact that it allows a court to force a recalcitrant husband to give his wife a deed of divorce despite the general rule that such a deed is only valid if given willingly.[11]

---

[10] Ecclesiastes 3:18–19.

[11] *Hilkhot Gerushin* 2:20.

In arguing that the will alone has the authority to obligate man to follow a particular code of conduct, Rabbi Berkovits must also explain why one would will himself to submit to an external author. When the external author's will is contrary to one's own reason, he will feel the need to suppress his self-evaluating desire so as to follow the external authority commensurate with the power of the authority's enforcement. Yet acting because of external force rather than from one's own will, as motivated by his true desires, is not ethical behavior but bondage. Rousseau explains in his *The Social Contract*, "If force compels obedience, there is no need to invoke a duty to obey, and if force ceases to compel obedience, there is no longer any obligation."[12] Only when one autonomously wills to act according to his own reason can his actions be judged as ethical. Rabbi Berkovits recognizes the need for man's autonomy for the existence of ethics, yet he must maintain that God is the absolute authority of religion. He is able to balance the contradictory needs of autonomy and external authority by the manner in which he describes God's relationship with man.

Rabbi Berkovits begins with the premise that in order for any relationship between God and man to exist, God must hide Himself and affirm man. If man were to be in the revealed presence of God, he would not survive, "for man shall not see Me and live."[13] He describes man's physical annihilation as follows:

> The Almighty is indeed 'a consuming fire;' not because he is angry with a sinful world, but because the potency of his being cannot be sustained by anything created. The Presence imperils men, not on account of God's will directed against man, but because divine nature is so charged with the vitality of being that its nearness naturally overwhelms all individual existence.[14]

[12] *The Social Contract*, 53.
[13] Exodus 33:20.
[14] *God, Man and History*, 33.

Even if man could physically survive a prophetic encounter of divine revelation, his standing as a moral being would still be lost. As seen above, man cannot be moral when he has no freedom of choice, yet the very fact of God's presence commands authoritatively. The Torah, for example, describes Moses's prophetic communication with God as being face to face, as a man speaks to his friend.[15] The imagery provokes the notion of friendship and a relationship based upon mutual respect and voluntary association. Yet the direct characterization of Moses is that he is God's slave.[16] As demonstrated by Moses's relationship with God, when man relates to a revealed God, the possibility of ethics is lost due to the vastly disparate levels of prominence in the relationship.

> Man is not a partner of God in the actuality of the I-Thou. He is altogether a creature, if ever there was one. As long as the actuality of the revelation lasts, man has no freedom. He cannot deny his Thou, he cannot disobey him. Only when the encounter has passed is he dismissed into a measure of self-hood and independence; only then can he deny and disobey.[17]

Therefore, religion cannot be a system of ethics if moral authority originates in the relationship between a revealed God and an invalidated man. In order to preserve the argument that religion is essentially divine ethics, Rabbi Berkovits separates the encounter of divine revelation from the continual relationship between God and man and argues that while the encounter is a necessary component to initiate religion, it is not the essential factor in religion's moral authority.

To explain the paradox of the divine encounter's necessity but preclusion from participating in authorizing divine ethics, it is essential to understand what the encounter accomplishes. The

---

[15] Exodus 33:11.

[16] Deuteronomy 34:5.

[17] *Major Themes*, 108.

experience of the encounter relates that the all-powerful, threatening God sustains man in order to relate to him. Rabbi Berkovits gives as an example the prophetic encounter of Ezekiel, in which the prophet relates, "I fell on my face. Then the spirit entered into me, and set me upon my feet, and spoke with me…."[18] The initial impact of the encounter physically threatened Ezekiel; only after God revived him and "set him upon his feet" was communication possible. The sages also describe a similar experience at the encounter at Sinai.

> Rabbi Yehoshua ben Levi also said: At every word which went forth from the mouth of the Holy One, blessed be He, the souls of Israel departed, for it is said, 'My soul went forth when he spoke.' But since their souls departed at the first word, how could they receive the second word? He brought down the dew with which He will resurrect the dead and revived them, as it is said, 'O God, You did send a plentiful rain, You confirmed Your inheritance, when it was weary.'[19]

God makes it possible for man to enter into a divine relationship, which signifies that God cares for him. The encounter also makes man cognizant of the idea that he is completely dependent on God and only "dust and ashes" before Him, yet because of God's affirmation, he still possesses value and dignity.[20]

Once the encounter informs man of God's concern, it must end in order to allow him to associate voluntarily with God. Anything besides the knowledge of God's existence and His desire for relationship that is communicated to man in the encounter has the power of absolute coercion, necessarily precluding it from being the basis of an ethical system. The sages recognized the coercive force of the encounter and its impediment to voluntary association in discussing the acceptance of the Torah at Sinai.

---

[18] Ezekiel 3:23–24.

[19] BT *Shabbat* 88b.

[20] *God, Man and History*, 38.

> 'And they stood under the mount': Rabbi Avdimi ben Hama ben Hasa said, 'This teaches that the Holy One, blessed be He, overturned the mountain upon them like an [inverted] cask, and said to them, If you accept the Torah, it will be well with you; if not, here shall be your burial.' Rabbi Aha ben Jacob observed, 'This furnishes a strong protest against the Torah [providing an excuse for non-observance, since it was forcibly imposed in the first place].' Said Raba, 'Yet even so, they accepted it once again in the days of Ahasuerus, for it is written: [the Jews] confirmed, and took upon them… they confirmed what they had accepted long before.'[21]

Only when God's presence is hidden can the Jewish people accept the Torah voluntarily. Therefore, even though Jewish history contains many prophetic encounters, they have only served to remind doubting Jews of the existence of the divine relationship.[22] Religion's basis for a true system of ethics lies in the relationship between a hidden God and an autonomous man.

> Religion does not reduce man to being a puppet of God; it elevates him to his highest dignity by enabling him to acknowledge God in free commitment. The 'fellowship' is initiated by God in the encounter; it is sustained after the encounter in the ever-renewed act of faith by man.[23]

The paradox of religion is that its foundation lies not in revelation, but rather in God's subsequent concealment.

---

[21] BT *Shabbat* 88a.

[22] See Maimonides, *Hilkhot Yesodei ha-Torah* 9:2, where he writes, "What is meant by the Torah's statement, 'I will appoint a prophet from among their brethren like you, and I will place My words in his mouth and he will speak?' He is not coming to establish a [new] faith, but rather to command the people [to fulfill] the precepts of the Torah and to warn against its transgression, as evidenced by the final prophet [Malachi], who proclaimed, 'Remember the Torah of Moses, My servant.'"

[23] *God, Man and History*, 50.

For the purposes of maintaining voluntary association, it is not enough for God only to hide Himself from man. He must conceal Himself from His entire creation. It would be futile to hide from man yet be made manifest to the rest of the world. One would be able to deduce God's existence as easily as one fills in a missing letter of a word written on a smudged piece of paper. To allow for free will, God must create a world that has the same affirmation and autonomy as that given to man. This can only be accomplished by creating an imperfect world. Arguing for its physical necessity, Rabbi Berkovits writes, "A faultless universe, devoid of evil, would not be distinguishable from the Creator; it would be one with him. In other words, it would not be a universe at all."[24] From a moral standpoint, even if the world runs by divine providence, chance must be seen as a feasible explanation of events for man to avoid holding the idea of strict determinism and shirking moral responsibility.[25]

While divine concealment allows for the possibility of free will and autonomy, it also allows for the existence of evil. Rabbi Berkovits explains the seeming contradiction between the creation of an imperfect world and God's declaration that it was good during the various stages of the process of creation by what he calls a philosophy of critical optimism.

> There is imperfection everywhere, but in everything that exists there is value as well. However, the full worth of reality is found not in its actual, but in its potential, value. God's creation is good because it is capable of goodness.[26]

God willed an imperfect world in order for man to willfully accept the absolute ethical obligation. In doing so, evil became a part of existence, yet only insofar as God remains hidden. Out of divine

---

[24] *God, Man and History*, 79.

[25] See BT *Berakhot* 33b where it states, "Rabbi Hanina further said: Everything is in the hand of heaven except the fear of heaven, as it says, And now, Israel, what does the Lord your God require of you but to fear."

[26] *God, Man and History*, 84.

concern, man is free to learn how to become an ethical being with the encouragement of knowing that God will perform a miracle to prevent total failure. God invites man to assist Him in running the world by revealing its latent goodness. In this manner, the moral scope of religion is much broader than a secular system of ethics. While secular ethics conveys to man how to act towards himself and others, religion informs man of his responsibility in both his own and the world's salvation.

The understanding of man's role in the divine relationship raises difficulties in Rabbi Berkovits's distinction in defining God's authority as absolute and society's authority as relative. Describing the nature of authority in secular ethics and in religion, he writes, "All secular ethics lack the quality of absolute obligation. They are as changeable as the desires and the wills that institute them; the law of God alone is as eternal as his will. Secular ethics, derived as it must be from a relative will, is subjective; God alone is the source of objectivity for all value and all law."[27] In Rabbi Berkovits's conception of authority, however, neither the external authority of secular ethics nor God's law is legitimate unless the individual voluntarily submits his will to it. Because a person's will is his true obligating authority, any other source of obligation must be considered as regental. It is not secular ethics that is fickle and admits of compromise for the sake of expediency. The fickle one is the person who no longer chooses to submit his will to secular ethics' authority, since he is compromising his ideals for the sake of base desires. Similarly, if religion is based upon the relationship between a hidden God and an autonomous man who voluntarily submits his will to God's will, how is the authority of religion any different from the authority of secular ethics? As long as man has freedom of will, neither the general will of society nor God's will has any true authority over man. To preserve the claim that God's will possesses absolute authority over man, Rabbi Berkovits would

---

[27] *God, Man and History*, 106.

be forced to argue for the inability of revocation once a person submits his will to an external authority. The absoluteness of obligation in religion would be due to God's eternality whereas the state is finite and politically vulnerable, and its authority dependent on external factors. However, choosing to maintain such an argument defeats its own purpose because ethics would be absent from either system, since no action subsequent to the initial submission can be considered voluntary and according to a self-reflecting will.

Rabbi Berkovits's second defense for restoring God and revelation as necessary for moral development is in his argument that regardless of whether reason possesses authority, it is powerless to compel man to engage in ethical conduct. Action, or intended physical movement, consists of cooperation between mind and body. Therefore, the body must be engaged in order to collaborate. In addition, the more ideal a given purpose, the more difficult it becomes for the body to overcome physical inertia in order to perform the act. Consistent with Maslow's hierarchy of needs, basic biological requirements, such as breathing and eating, take little, if any, mental prompting for the body to act. Performing acts which insure safety and security require more cognition and physical preparation. As one attempts to fulfill needs of higher moral import, such as love and belonging, esteem, and, ultimately, self-actualization, it becomes much harder for the mind to overcome the body's physical inertia to take action. Moreover, if the action required is outside the body's normal range of movement, the mind may have even greater difficulty in directing the body to act contrary to its own nature.

> At the core of human existence is the source of man's ethical dilemma. Man, taking his place in the realm of the spirit as well as of matter, is committed to ethical action. He is obligated to meet the other, the non-self, in a relationship of caring involvement. But he can do this only through the

> instrumentality of a physical organism which is in essence under the sway of laws of self-centeredness.[28]

Reason is only one part of a person's make-up; it cannot succeed alone in making man ethical. Man must engage his body, which is inclined solely towards survival and pleasure, to become not only acquiescent but willing, as it were, to act ethically. For mind and body to consistently cooperate in the performance of ethical actions, man must treat ethics as he would a skill. He must train his body so that ethical action becomes second nature.

Training requires both repetitive action and the ability to make mistakes during the learning process that would have little consequence. Practice allows the body to become accustomed to a new type of activity, so that when it counts, the required action is performed properly. Rabbi Berkovits identifies the ritual laws as providing the proper prescriptive and inhibitive training; they are commanded only to provide man with repetitive exercises in inconsequential circumstances so that he can practice acting according to religious directives. They create artificial environments in which the obligation or prohibition is arbitrary, yet not a complete submission of the body, so that the body may become accustomed to performing or refraining when confronted with a real ethical challenge.

Rabbi Berkovits stops short of arguing that the ritual laws are only the "handmaiden of ethics." While they do make ethical action second nature for the body, they also train man to worship God with his whole being by fulfilling a divine command. Under the guidance of the ritual law, man is able to transform even the most physical experiences into a spiritual expression of the divine relationship.

> The Jew who, in submission to God, satisfies his hunger by curbing the self-centeredness of an organic impulse has succeeded in serving God, even by the purely material

[28] *God, Man and History*, 108.

> activity of keeping his body alive. Even when eating, he lives in the presence of God. 'Blessed are you, Eternal our God, who brings forth bread from the earth,' the blessing a Jew says before eating bread, is not only a form of divine service, but also encourages man's enjoyment of bread as God's creation. The enjoyment itself, essentially biological, becomes oriented to God, because the blessing prepares for it spiritually.[29]

In unifying the mind and the body for the purpose of divine worship, the harmonization of human nature is achieved, whereby the mind guides the body and the body executes the will of the mind. The materialization of the spirit and the spiritualization of the body is what Rabbi Berkovits calls holiness. Religion and secular ethics are thus no longer seen as competing moral systems. The holy man of religion is an ethical man, yet his actions also enable him to wholly relate to God.

In relation to the telos of history, however, religion does take a back seat to ethics. Quoting the rabbinic dictum that the Torah was given to purify mankind,[30] Rabbi Berkovits infers this to be the only reason the Torah was given. Once mankind has reached the pinnacle of ethics, the Torah will no longer be relevant. Man will act ethically not due to divine authority, but only because he desires to do so. He writes, "Only through the law will the law be overcome. When that phase is reached, mankind will have fulfilled its destiny, and history will be at an end."[31] Without venturing into a discussion about the eternality of the Torah, a tenet debated in the many disputations throughout Jewish history, the idea that the Torah is significant only when man is still unethical undermines the value of the divine relationship and diminishes the concept of holiness in fulfilling the commandments. In Rabbi Berkovits's theory of ritual law, man performs the ritual commands by divine decree, but also

---

[29] *God, Man and History*, 127.
[30] *God, Man and History*, 133.
[31] *God, Man and History*, 134.

because he believes that their fulfillment will train him to become ethical. Primacy of focus, whether inward towards moral improvement or outwards towards relating to the divine, will depend on which reason for fulfilling the commandment has priority. If the Torah is to be overcome when man perfects himself morally, then serving God is only an intermediate step until one can serve his own will, which makes the divine relationship one of expediency. Because ethics is the primary motive, man will primarily focus inward during the performance of a ritual act rather than outward to the divine authority that commands it. By the end of history, when the Torah is overcome, not only will holy actions no longer exist, but awareness of the Wholly Other will not either.

Ethical training, or habituation, as a method of moral development originated with Aristotle and found a place in religious thought with Maimonides. Rabbi Berkovits modifies both the Aristotelian manner in which habituation renders the body amenable to moral prescriptions and Maimonides's religious focus toward which actions are to be directed. It is in his originality that the widely appreciated theory of habituation encounters objection.

In his *Nicomachean Ethics*, Aristotle argues that man has no innate moral inclination; he only has the propensity to acquire ethical virtues by making ethical conduct a habit.[32] Aristotelian moral training, however, differs from the way Rabbi Berkovits suggests ritual law promotes moral development. According to Rabbi Berkovits, the ritual commandments serve only an indirect function. Ritual prohibitions facilitate sublimation of desire, while prescriptive ritual commandments create a type of ethical muscle memory. The rituals have no intrinsic moral value.

On the other hand, Aristotle advocates a direct method of ethical training in which the actions that habituate man to become ethical are, in essence, ethical ones when they are performed by an ethical person.[33] Repetitive conduct reinforces the virtues associated

---

[32] *Nicomachean Ethics*, 18.
[33] *Nicomachean Ethics*, 20.

with it, making ethical action more difficult for someone who has acquired bad habits from repeated immoral actions, and easier for someone with a good character. Habituation does not just train the body to act in the way that the mind already knows is right; rather, development of moral character and moral judgment are interdependent. In describing moral character, he writes, "For it is not merely the state in accord with the correct reason, but the state involving the correct reason… we cannot be fully good without prudence, or prudent without virtue of character."[34] Repetitive practice does not make perfect. Rather, a person must learn from each ethical act to better apply the lessons learned to the next situation. This process does not make ethical action a conditioned reflex but rather a response that reflects an understanding of the scenario. With experience, ethical action becomes more and more accurate in responding properly to different moral dilemmas. An Aristotelian retort to Rabbi Berkovits's comparison of ethics to a skill would be that it is correct that one does not learn how to swim by reading a book about swimming techniques, or learn to paint by contemplating artistic styles,[35] but neither does one learn to swim by sublimating the desire to run in order to express it in swimming, nor does one learn to paint by learning to eat with chopsticks. The author of the *Sefer ha-Hinukh* expresses the idea that religious character results from religious action, and that even ritual commandments have direct influence, in his answer regarding why there are so many ritual commandments in remembrance of the exodus from Egypt.

> Know that a person develops according to his actions. His heart and his thoughts constantly reflect the deeds in which he engages, whether good or bad. Even a person who is completely wicked in his heart, that every imagination of the thoughts of his heart is nothing but evil all the time, if his spirit is awakened and he endeavors to engage

[34] *Nicomachean Ethics*, 98–99.
[35] *God, Man and History*, 112.

> persistently in Torah and the commandments, even if not with proper intent, he will immediately be inclined toward goodness and the force of his actions will eradicate his evil inclination, since a person's actions direct the focus of the heart. Even a completely righteous person whose heart is honest and innocent, desiring [to learn] Torah and [to perform] the commandments – if perchance he were to engage constantly in tainted matters, as if to say for example that the king forced him and appointed him to an evil position, if all his actions were directed towards this position, in truth, eventually his righteousness would leave him and he would become completely wicked, since it is a known matter and the truth that all men develop characters according to their actions.[36]

One may also challenge the indirect influence of the ritual law as follows: there may be no guarantee that just because a man masters the training exercises, he will be ready to perform properly when it counts. Success or failure could only be determined if and when he is faced with an ethical dilemma. Until that time arises, fulfillment of the ritual laws cannot be said to make a person righteous, since they have no ethical power in and of themselves to reinforce a correct moral perspective.

Although Maimonides agrees with Aristotle that a person develops moral virtues by repetitive moral action which accustoms him to be moral,[37] he rejects his belief in a reciprocal process of education between reason and the body in learning how to be ethical. Instead, Maimonides holds that the commandments provide man with the guidelines to become moral by directing his behavior towards the ethical mean. Unlike Aristotle, where moral perfection is contingent upon laws prescribing a proper moral upbringing, whereby morality will always be at the mercy of human

[36] *Sefer ha-Hinukh,* Commandment 16.
[37] *Hilkhot Deot* 1:7; *Ethical Writings of Maimonides*, 68 (*Shemonah Perakim*, Chapter 4).

miscalculation and error,[38] the eternal perfection of the Torah is absolute and will not condition man towards a relative morality.[39] Similarly to Rabbi Berkovits, he admits that, if not for the Torah's command, the ritual law would have no moral relevance;[40] however, unlike Rabbi Berkovits, lack of moral relevance does not negate its inherent importance and direct influence on character development. About the ritual commandments, Maimonides puts forth, "They always say with regard to the verse: *For it is no vain thing – and if it is vain, it is because of you,* meaning that this legislation is not a vain matter without a useful end and that if it seems to you that this is the case with regard to some of the commandments, the deficiency resides in your apprehension."[41] The significance of the ritual law, for Maimonides, is in obedience and not in the sublimation of desire or honing of the body; when a person obeys a ritual command, he concomitantly embraces yet sacrifices his own desire and deliberately pushes his inert body to perform the deed.

> They said: The reward is according to the pain. Even more significant is their commanding a man to be continent and their forbidding him to say: 'I would not naturally yearn to commit this transgression, even if it were not prohibited by the Law.' This is what they say: Rabban Shimon ben Gamliel says: Let not a man say, 'I do not want to eat meat with milk, I do not want to wear mixed fabric, I do not want to have illicit sexual relations,' but [let him say] 'I want to, but what shall I do – my Father in heaven has forbidden me.'[42]

---

38 *Nicomachean Ethics*, 168–169.

39 See the fourth chapter of the *Shemonah Perakim* where Maimonides writes, "The Law forbids what it forbids and commands what it commands only for this reason, i.e., that we move away from one side as a means of discipline." (*Ethical Writings of Maimonides*, 71)

40 *Ethical Writings of Maimonides*, 80 (*Shemonah Perakim*, chapter 6).

41 *Guide for the Perplexed*, 507.

42 *Ethical Writings of Maimonides*, 79 (*Shemonah Perakim*, chapter 6).

Although Halakha contains many commandments that we judge as ethical and does influence moral development through habituation, the significance of Halakha is not in its ethical training. Halakha's purpose is to enable man to direct all his thoughts and actions toward the sole goal of perceiving God to the best of his ability.[43] A flawed moral character does not even hinder man from reaching the heights of divine awareness, as Maimonides explains: "To possess the moral virtues in their entirety, to the extent of not being impaired by any vice at all, is not one of the conditions of prophecy."[44] According to Maimonides, moral development is not the primary concern for Halakha, as Rabbi Berkovits contends. It is only a consequence due to the overlap between ethics and religion.[45]

While Rabbi Berkovits defends the need for religion by denying rationality the authority and power to form an effective system of ethics, he feels that reason is paramount in the development of Halakha. Rabbi Berkovits differentiates between Halakha and the Law by defining Halakha as the Law applied in a given situation. It gives the Torah life by applying the spirit of the Law's principles

---

43 *Ethical Writings of Maimonides*, 75 (*Shemonah Perakim*, chapter 5).

44 *Ethical Writings of Maimonides*, 81 (*Shemonah Perakim*, chapter 7).

45 One must be aware that Maimonides's contention that moral perfection is not the primary concern of Halakha does not mean that Maimonides does not believe that one need not act in a manner that can be perceived as a moral. What differs is the reason for such action. In his discussion regarding the four levels of perfection, he describes the third level, moral perfection, as a disposition that is useful in interpersonal relations. One acts morally, therefore, because it is the right way to act in society. Its relativity is revealed when one is alone. Maimonides writes, "For if you suppose a human individual is alone, acting on no one, you will find that all his moral virtues are in vain and without employment and unneeded, and that they do not perfect the individual in anything; for he only needs them and they again become useful to him in regard to someone else." (*Guide*, 635) When man attains intellectual perfection, whereby he acquires the rational virtues, every action is in service to God since all action is performed in the context of *imitatio Dei*. Therefore, although the same interpersonal action may be performed, the intrinsic value of the act differs when done with a moral reason or with a religious reason.

and values to prescriptive action in the world.[46] At Sinai, the Jewish people received the Law from God, yet the Law is an ideal that needs not only a basis in reality but an adapting basis for a constantly changing world.

> Halakha is the bridge over which Torah enters reality, with the capacity to shape it meaningfully and in keeping with its own intention. Halakha is the technique of Torah-application to a concrete contemporary situation. But while the Torah is eternal, the concrete historic situation is forever changing. Halakha therefore, as the application of Torah in a given situation, will forever uncover new levels of Torah-depth and Torah-meaning and thus make new facets of Judaism visible.[47]

God's revelation at Sinai did not make known God's absolute essence, nor was God's absolute word communicated. Just as God's presence was revealed in a manner that human beings could tolerate, God's word was given in a manner that humans could understand, as the sages say, "The Torah speaks in the language of man." After receiving the Torah, it became man's responsibility to "humanize" it, by which Rabbi Berkovits means to take into consideration human nature and historical context when applying Torah values to various situations. He claims that the obligation to humanize the Torah is the ultimate meaning behind Rabbi Yehoshua's declaration that the Torah is not in Heaven.[48]

When one humanizes the Torah, he imposes his own rationality upon the divine law in order to create legislation that is consistent with his own understanding of which Torah values should be applied in a given context. The first level of humanization is to understand that the Torah was given at a particular moment in the historical progression of ethical development. Therefore, the Torah must tolerate certain disagreeable behavior until the time that man

---

[46] *Crisis and Faith*, 85.
[47] "Authentic Judaism and Halakha," 72.
[48] *Not in Heaven*, 73.

matures and will no longer accept that type of conduct. In his discussion of the laws relating to marriage and the status of women, Rabbi Berkovits states that there are three distinct phases of Torah guidance: Torah-tolerated, Torah-established, and Torah-taught, where each stage is less influenced by the mores, conditions, and circumstances of society than the previous one.[49] He opines that all negative statements about women in the Talmud and their corresponding Halakha are not Torah values, but rather are Torah-tolerated values that reflect the broader society in Talmudic times. He writes, "In attempting to understand this strange phenomenon in Jewish life, we must realize that many of the negative opinions about women and their place in society are not authentically Jewish. For example, a study of the practices in classical Greece reveals many similarities and parallels between the two societies."[50] Rabbi Berkovits supports his claim of a layered system of Torah guidance by quoting Maimonides's view of the reason why sacrifices were commanded despite the superiority of prayer as a form of worship. I will quote his reading of Maimonides, since it summarizes his position quite clearly.

> It is impossible for man to change suddenly from one extreme to the other. It is impossible for him suddenly to give up what he has been accustomed to. As God sent Moses to make us 'a kingdom of priests and a holy nation,' and to dedicate ourselves to His service, as it is said, 'And to serve Him with all your heart,' the prevailing custom in the world was to sacrifice animals in the temples which people had erected to their idols, to bow down to them and burn incense before them, etc. God's wisdom counseled Him that to command the Jews to give up all that kind of service and annul it completely would have been something that their hearts could not have accepted. Human nature is forever inclined towards the accustomed practice. Such a command would be as if a prophet came to us [today] to

---

49 *Jewish Women in Time and Torah*, 1.
50 *Jewish Women in Time and Torah*, 25.

> call us to the service of God and said, 'God has commanded you not to pray to Him or fast or ask for help in times of trouble, but to make your service be pure thought without action.' [In fact, this is what Maimonides considered the *avodah ahronah*, the ultimate service of God by pure thought meditating upon Him.] For this reason, God allowed the [generally practiced] sacrificial services to remain, but directed them away from those created or imagined powers in which there is no truth to His own name, blessed be He, and commanded to dedicate them to Him. Thus, He commanded us to build a sanctuary to Him, etc., and that the sacrifices shall be offered to Him, 'If one from among you will offer a sacrifice unto Me,' etc., etc. Thus, this divine guidance achieved its purpose – that even the memory of idol worship was erased among us, and the important truth was established in the midst of our people, i.e., the existence of God and His unity.[51]

The Torah's tolerance in allowing man to develop gradually into a moral being is not only seen in the realm of gender and the sacrificial cult, but also within the socio-economic sphere. Like sacrifices, slavery was a prevalent practice during the time of the Bible. However, while general society considered slaves as mere chattel, the Torah allowed slavery but imposed moral conditions upon the master, who was commanded to treat his Canaanite slave with mercy and justice. Enslavement of a Jew was only permitted in the event that he could not make restitution for his theft and would thereby have to repay his debt by working. He could only be enslaved for a maximum term of six years, at the end of which he would be paid a severance fee. If he could save enough money to pay his debt, he could go free. Although legally he was a slave, he must be treated like a hired servant in terms of the type of work he was obligated to perform and like an equal in terms of providing him food, clothing and living conditions. Given the restrictions on

[51] *Jewish Women in Time and Torah*, 30. *Guide for the Perplexed* 3:32.

the practice of slavery, Rabbi Berkovits states, "There is little doubt in my mind that in a Jewish state, governed by these teachings and rules, had it been in existence, slavery would have been abolished long before the age of Lincoln."[52] In all realms of life, the Torah accepts man as he is at that particular moment in time, while giving him the proper guidance for him to grow, on his own, in order to actualize his own moral potential.

Humanization also occurs when the rabbis recognize that the practice of a particular commandment conflicts with general Torah ideals and use legal innovation to remove the impediment to the spirit of the Law. Rabbi Berkovits gives numerous examples of rabbinic leniency in marital law that seemingly contradict the simple understanding of what the Torah law should be in order to prevent women from becoming *agunot* or from remaining in marriages that have become intolerable. In some instances, the rabbis even go so far as to assume the power to annul a legally valid marriage retroactively. Although Rabbi Berkovits recognizes that there are legal justifications for the rabbinic abrogation,[53] he explains that the moral reason is the real impetus behind the legal action. In defense of rabbinic innovation, he writes, "The reason seems to be that the laws of *kiddushin* do not represent the entire Torah. Apart from the right of the husband over divorce, there is another commandment, even more comprehensive and compelling: 'And thou shall love thy neighbor as thyself.' It could not be disregarded. There was a conflict between two laws of the Torah. A solution had to be found, and it was found. Its promulgation required a great deal of courage and a deep sense of rabbinical responsibility."[54] Rabbinic legal leniency that results from moral sensitivity is also found in the laws of purity. One example Rabbi Berkovits gives is the negation of ritual purity standards during the festival celebration. When the Temple existed, Jews were expected to make pilgrimage there on

[52] *Jewish Women in Time and Torah*, 33.
[53] See *Not in Heaven* and "The Nature of Halakhic Authority."
[54] *Jewish Women in Time and Torah*, 49.

the three festivals. When *amei ha-aretz*, those who were ignorant of the Torah and suspected of not being careful regarding ritual purity, came to the Temple grounds and bought food and other provisions, they inevitably handled goods in the shops and markets, rendering them unfit to eat by those who abided by the purity laws. Rabbi Berkovits states that the rabbis suspended the laws of purity during this time not in order to allow everyone to buy the possibly defiled goods and thereby protect the economy. Rather, they did so in order to avoid causing public insult to their fellow Jews, regardless of their level of knowledge.[55]

The exercise of judicial review to uproot laws that contradict Torah ideals is not only employed for those ideals traditionally considered moral. The rabbis held Halakha to the standard of allowing an effectively functioning economy as well. According to the Torah, all private debts must be forfeited during *shemittah,* the Sabbatical year. When Hillel realized that Jews would no longer lend money for fear that loans would not be repaid before *shemittah*, he weighed the value of the Torah's obligation to protect the poor, who no longer could receive financial support, and the interests of a strong economy for the security of the Jewish community. He found a legal method, the *prosbul*, for transforming private debts into public debts, which are not cancelled by *shemittah*.[56] Rabbi Berkovits recognizes a similarity between the conflict in the time of Hillel and the conflict arising from the agriculture requirements of *shemittah* in an international economic community and intimates that there is a need for a legal abrogation of *shemittah* observance in a manner that incorporates the Torah values that the commandment of *shemittah* teaches.[57]

The third form of rabbinic humanization occurs within the halakhic derivation of particular laws. Rabbi Berkovits gives many examples where *sevara*, or what he calls common sense or pragmatic

---

[55] *Not in Heaven*, 23.
[56] *Crisis and Faith*, 86.
[57] *Not in Heaven*, 100.

truth,[58] dominates the halakhic process. He shows how common sense can have validity equivalent to that of a biblical statement, may suppress the plain meaning of a biblical text, and may even limit the power of a biblical injunction by exempting situations where the law would be considered unacceptable.[59] The sound reasoning of a single individual can even overrule the popular opinion, despite the general biblical injunction to rule according to the majority.[60]

Although traditional rabbinic authority allows for the Torah to stay contemporary, successful halakhic development through humanization has been obstructed by the fossilization of Halakha. The rabbis may have saved the Oral Torah as it reflected the Halakha of their time by writing it down, yet because the Torah must be continually transformed in order to be applicable in every period in history, they saved the Halakha of the moment at the expense of that of the future. Rabbi Berkovits writes:

> When the spoken word was forced into the straightjacket of a written mould it was an unavoidable violation of the essence of Halakha. It was no one's fault; nevertheless, it was a spiritual calamity of the first magnitude. Orthodoxy is, in a sense, Halakha in a straightjacket.[61]

The only way to rescue Halakha from stagnation, Rabbi Berkovits suggests, is to return the Oral Torah to its original intent. Today's rabbis must recognize that current situations are different from ones that occurred in the past, and minority opinions should have more legal strength today than yesteryear. In allowing for a wider range of legal precedent, Rabbi Berkovits suggests relying on minority opinions from the *aharonim* to the *tannaim*, so that one could better apply Halakha, and the values of the Torah, to the modern era. In such an event, the particular rulings of Halakha may

[58] *Not in Heaven*, 79.
[59] *Not in Heaven*, 6.
[60] *Not in Heaven*, 7.
[61] *Crisis and Faith*, 95.

change but Halakha, as the application of Torah ideals to the modern world, will be strengthened.

His boldest support for the superiority of man's reason lies in his reading of the Talmudic story of the oven of Akhnai. In brief, there was a disagreement between Rabbi Eliezer and the majority of the sages regarding the purity of an oven. Rabbi Eliezer ruled that it was impure and, after a number of miracles occurred to show that he was correct, a heavenly voice proclaimed, "What is it you want with Rabbi Eliezer? Wherever he expresses an opinion, Halakha goes according to him." Rabbi Yehoshua answered, "It is not in Heaven," whereupon the sages ruled that the oven was pure. In a discussion of the event afterwards, God is reported to have said laughingly, "My sons have defeated me."[62] Certainly this story leaves the reader with the idea that man determines Halakha, and his own rationality is the final judge for how Torah values should be applied to the world. Yet the story of the oven of Akhnai is not the only story in which a heavenly voice proclaims Halakha. The Talmud relates,

> For three years there was a dispute between the House of Shammai and the House of Hillel, the former asserting, 'Halakha is in agreement with our views,' and the latter contending, 'Halakha is in agreement with our views.' Then a heavenly voice announced, 'These and those are the words of the living God, but Halakha is in accord with the rulings of the House of Hillel.'[63]

Since the House of Hillel was greater in number and the House of Shammai was greater in intellect, each side argued that its perspective should be the one to determine Halakha. Although the Talmud gives further justification for the decision to rule according to the House of Hillel, the proclamation of the heavenly voice is acknowledged as determining the decision.[64] Also, every mention of

---

[62] BT *Bava Metzia* 59b.
[63] BT *Eruvin* 13b, *Gittin* 6b.
[64] BT *Berakhot* 51b.

Rabbi Yehoshua's assertive declaration in the Talmud is used to support following the School of Shammai's legal decisions[65] or to explain why it must be stated specifically that Halakha accords with the House of Hillel – for fear that because of Rabbi Yehoshua's statement, one might follow the House of Shammai despite the heavenly voice.[66] In the Jerusalem Talmud, Rabbi Yehoshua's bold retort to the heavenly voice loses its defiant confidence since Rabbi Eliezer recognized that the majority establishes Halakha.[67] Given these two contradictory accounts, how can one reconcile Rabbi Berkovits's claim that the Torah is no longer in Heaven but is for man to humanize, with some possible influence from the heavenly voice on halakhic decision-making?

The Tosafists recognize the contradiction between accepting the heavenly voice in favor of the House of Hillel and rejecting its opinion that Halakha accords with Rabbi Eliezer. They resolve the ostensible contradiction by stating that in the case where the heavenly voice was accepted, it only assisted in preventing an erroneous understanding of a Torah directive, but it did not rule on the dispute itself.[68] Just as the heavenly voice did not render a ruling on which school would determine Halakha, Rabbi Yehoshua's statement that the Torah is not in Heaven did not decide Halakha either, as seen from the other cases in which his statement is mentioned. Rather, Rabbi Jeremiah's rewording of Rabbi Yehoshua gives his statement legal grounding "that the Torah had already been given at Mount Sinai. We pay no attention to a heavenly voice because You wrote long ago in the Torah at Mount Sinai that one must incline after the majority."[69] Halakha is determined neither by

---

[65] BT *Eruvin* 7a, *Hullin* 44a, *Yevamot* 14a.
[66] BT *Pesahim* 114a, *Berakhot* 52a.
[67] JT *Moed Katan* 3:1.
[68] Tosafot *Hullin* 44a; Tosafot *Bava Metzia* 59b; Tosafot *Yevamot* 14a; Tosafot *Eruvin* 6b; Tosafot *Pesahim* 114a; *Igrot Moshe, Orah Hayyim* 1:15.
[69] BT *Bava Metzia* 59b.

divine intervention nor by prophecy,[70] neither is it established by man's rationality alone. It is determined by the rules of halakhic derivation that the Torah itself imposes on the jurist to apply when making a halakhic decision. While it is true that a judge can only rule according to what he sees with his own eyes, the intention of this statement is that he must consider both the reality of the case before him and his understanding of proper Torah jurisprudence when reaching a decision. The judge should not come with his own preconceived notions to find halakhic justification for what he has already determined, but should base his decision on the juridical method prescribed by the Torah.

Upon deeper analysis of Rabbi Berkovits's examples of halakhic humanization, it seems as if they may not support his belief in man's ability to distill Torah values, leaving commandments behind and reinterpreting laws during his moral progression through history. As stated above, the purpose that Maimonides assigned to the sacrifices identifies them as a stepping stone to prayer, which is deemed the ideal way to fulfill the commandment of worshipping God.[71] Because of their secondary purpose, the manner in which sacrifices could be performed according to Halakha was limited. Nevertheless, the obligation of sacrifices was never abrogated completely in favor of prayer. In his *Book of the Commandments*, Maimonides enumerates prayer as the fulfillment of the specific commandment of worshipping God. Yet he also enumerates each commandment of the sacrificial rite even though they could have been included in the general category since they are considered only a way-station on the path to proper worship. Their enumeration shows that as specific commandments, the performance of sacrifices is eternally valid, as is the rest of the Torah.

Rabbi Berkovits's praise for what he understands as rabbinic courage in finding legal ways to uproot obligations that impede society's moral progress actually ignores the moral situation that

---

[70] *Hilkhot Yesodei ha-Torah* 9:4.
[71] *Guide for the Perplexed*, 527.

required such legal machinations. Hillel's *prosbul* was necessary not because the economy surpassed the traditional market economy, becoming a market of financial engineering that was dependent upon a lending system. People were simply not lending to their poorer fellow Jews for fear of losing their money. Self-centeredness at the expense of society damaged the economy to the point that Hillel was forced to take legal action.

Similarly, the rabbinic preference for *halitza* over *yibbum* did not stem from a desire to release childless women from the obligation of marrying their deceased husbands' brothers. *Halitza* became the dominant practice to avoid the improper performance *yibbum*, since people were seeking to marry for their own selfish motives and not to carry on the deceased's name. Furthermore, when the Temple existed, the sages did not suspend purity laws because they condoned the laxity of the masses. They had to take measures so the masses would come to the Temple. As to Rabbi Berkovits's suggestion for reforming the laws of *shemittah*, in what way could the ideals of *shemittah* be implemented in a society which is dangerously alienated from nature, when the very idea of *shemittah* in general focuses on how Jews perceive their relationship to the land? Rather than condoning the ethical failings of today by finding legal justifications for society's weakness, true rabbinic courage would be to instill ideal Torah values into society so that legal loopholes would no longer be necessary.

In his discussion of the power of reason to shape the particulars of Halakha, Rabbi Berkovits gives as an example Rabbi Yosi's ability to overrule a majority. In a case of granting power of attorney to another person by merely word of mouth sent to him by a messenger, Rabbi Yosi alone rules that it is not effective. When Rabbi Shimon questions Rabbi's ruling in favor of Rabbi Yosi, he responds, "Be quiet, my son, be quiet. Had you known Rabbi Yosi personally, you would realize that he always has his reasons for his opinion."[72] From this example, Rabbi Berkovits makes the general

[72] *Not in Heaven*, 7; BT *Gittin* 67a.

claim that Halakha is decided by a lone opinion if that particular sage's reasoning is more convincing than that of the majority. Yet there is another passage in which Rabbi Yosi's acumen is recognized, yet does not overrule the majority. In a disagreement about the quality of supervisors for ritual slaughter, Rabbi Yosi rules stringently against a majority. The Talmud relates:

> Rabbi Hananel reported in the name of Rav, 'Halakha is not in accordance with Rabbi Yosi.' Surely this is obvious, for 'Where a single opinion is opposed to the opinion of more than one, the law follows the latter!' You might have thought that we must adopt Rabbi Yosi's opinion because he is known to have deep reasons [for his rulings]. He therefore informs us [that it is not so].[73]

Although Rabbi Berkovits gives another example in order to prove the power of reason in deciding Halakha, his proof does the opposite. As in the previous example, the Talmud declares that Halakha does not accord with the opinion of a certain rabbi. The necessity for such a declaration is that the minority opinion is so convincing that one might think, mistakenly, that it is Halakha.[74] If the Talmud must declare specifically that Halakha rules against the more rational decision, would that not show that reason is not the ultimate litmus test for halakhic decision-making?

Although man plays a significant role in applying the Torah to the world through the halakhic process, his role remains in the realm of application and does not venture into the realm of definition. Rabbinic legislation has both expanded and limited biblical commandments, and halakhic decisions have been more or less conciliatory, depending on the particular case and general circumstances in which the rule was made. However, the freedom and the responsibility that a halakhic decisor has to effect change does not rest on his rational capacity nor on his understanding of

---

[73] BT *Bekhorot* 37a.

[74] *Not in Heaven*, 7; BT *Shabbat* 60b.

society's moral state. His halakhic authority stems solely from his knowledge of Halakha and its jurisprudence, gained from a strong appreciation of the Torah tradition, and his ability to reconcile new disputes and problems by drawing upon his knowledge and experience in previous cases. Rabbi Sherira Gaon summarizes this person's qualifications as follows:

> [He] is considered as Rabbi Nahman was in his generation, an expert in Mishna and Talmud, as well as in balanced thinking. He has many years of legal research and has been sufficiently tested and passed without error.[75]

Only one who has internalized the Torah and appreciates the gravity of his responsibility in applying it to everyday life can be considered qualified to represent man's role in the halakhic process. Having a keen intellect and the ability to manipulate various legal precedents to reach a favorable outcome does not make a Torah scholar. The current moral situation of society should not determine Halakha; rather, Halakha, and the history of the Jewish tradition, should seek to improve society.

Religion can never be equated with ethics or Halakha with ethical maxims simply because the source of content in religion, as opposed to solely the source of authority, is not the same as in ethics. Halakha and Torah are manifestations of God's wisdom, which man could never understand by man's reason alone, "For My thoughts are not your thoughts, nor are your ways My ways, says the Lord."[76] While there is an overlap between religion and ethics, in that certain commandments may be perceived as ethical, the Torah advises us not to see the fulfillment of the commandments simply as an ethical act.[77] In differentiating between natural,

---

[75] Tur, *Hoshen Mishpat,* Chapter 3.

[76] Isaiah 55:8.

[77] Throughout Leviticus, every instance where the Jews are warned about following the *Mishpatim* (rational commandments), they are similarly warned regarding the *Hukim* (ritual commandments), and the verse invariably concludes

societal, and divine law, Rabbi Josef Albo makes the following distinction:

> The intention of natural law is to remove the yoke [of immorality] and draw one near to righteousness in order that men are distanced from stealing, robbery and murder, so that there is friendship between men and everyone is safe from violent anarchy. The intention of societal law is to remove that which is indecent and to attract that which is pleasant so that men are removed from public indecency. This is superior to natural [law], because societal [law] will also improve men and will create an environment where society is reformed just as natural [law reforms individuals]. The intention of divine law is to ameliorate man to attain true success, which is spiritual success and immortality. [It is designed] to show them the way to achieve it, and to inform them of true goodness so they will endeavor towards this goal. [It] also [will] inform them of true evil so they will protect themselves from it, and [will] condition [men] to avoid imaginary paths [towards the true goal] so that they will not be enticed and suffer from them. It also places them on the right path to improve society through civility and peace so that society will not engage in evil since it recognizes true success. Also, [men] will not be detoured from trying to attain their final goal by those who imagine [that they posses] the divine law. It is in this way that [divine] is superior to societal law.[78]

To conflate religion and ethics, while giving credit to man for his own edification, limits both the role of the divine and the scope of man's responsibility. The Talmud relates that the nations have wisdom but not the Torah. One must not devalue what the Jewish people possess or the unique position they have in history. Through the study and practice of the Torah, a person accomplishes much

---

with recognition of God or the covenant between God and Israel. See Leviticus 18:4–5, 19:37, 20:22, 25:18, 26:15.

[78] *Sefer ha-Ikarim,* Section 1, Chapter 7.

more than learning proper behavior in order to make the world good in man's eyes. He creates a dwelling place for the Divine Presence and becomes a partner with God in the creation of the world.

CONCLUSION

IN ORDER TO LEAD a generation of Orthodox Jews who live in the modern world, the Modern Orthodox thinker must know his audience. He must use a language that people understand and analogies to which they can relate. If he does not place the Torah values and priorities that he desires to impart in the context of the lives of his students, he will be unable to portray the Torah as a living system or Halakha as applicable. The era in which Rabbis Soloveitchik and Berkovits began their rabbinical careers in America is described by Charles Liebman as follows:

> The evidence suggests an absence of religious as distinct from ethnic commitment on the part of most nominally Orthodox immigrants to the United States. Thus, the rise of Conservative Judaism and secularism in American Jewish life did not entail a decision to opt out of traditional religion. It was, rather, a decision to substitute new social and cultural mores for the older ones, which had been intermingled with certain ritual manifestations.[1]

If during this time the American Orthodox community lacked a strong traditional Jewish background, the only way to convey a traditional Jewish message was to put it into the modern terminology that people were using to understand the world around them. The benefit of translating traditional Jewish concepts, of which many contemporary Jews were only superficially aware, into a language that could be easily understood given the contemporary

---

[1] "Orthodoxy in American Jewish Life," 30.

cultural milieu outweighed the risk of any interpretative slanting that translation in general necessitates.

Today, when we teach our children so that they may grow up to be self-reflecting Jews living according to traditional concepts and able to understand their way of life vis-à-vis the world around them, which language should we use to impart those values? Gone is the ability to ignore the modern framework; the world is too integrated and complex for anyone to create a conception of it without considering the philosophical consequences of all he must encounter on a daily basis. However, one will conceive of Orthodox Judaism in a modern world differently depending on whether the modern world provides content or context.

The Modern Orthodox thinker's aim today should be to recognize the tendency for divergence when translating Jewish concepts into a modern mode of expression and to understand that modern interpretations may actually be new ideas rather than new descriptions of old ideas. Today's thinker must be cognizant of the risk of divergence and if faced with such must decide which definition will be primary and which will take a subordinate position. In other words, he will have to decide how modern or how orthodox his thought will be.

Given the great responsibility of finding a language to communicate the values of Judaism in a modern world, one would be wise to remember the words of Avtalyon, "Sages, be careful with your words, for you may be exiled and sent to a place of bad waters. Then students who come to you will drink and die, and it will be a desecration of the name of Heaven." Be careful when expressing your ideas not to leave room for doubt and misinterpretation. Because people will take heed of your choice of language and not consider your words as mere casual remarks, you must make sure that those who hear them will not fall to error. For if the waters of life that is the Torah are rendered into the bad waters of incorrect belief and then are drunken by future generations, you will find that the name of Heaven will be lost through its assimilation of foreign content. As noted by the son of David, king of Israel, the manner in which we teach Judaism to our children will be the manner in which they live it.

חנך לנער על פי דרכו גם כי יזקין לא יסור ממנה (משלי כב:ו)

Educate the lad according to his way.
Even when he grows old, he will not swerve from it.
(Proverbs 22:6)

BIBLIOGRAPHY

Anscombe, G.E.M. *Intention*. Cambridge: Harvard University Press, 2000.

Aristotle. *Nicomachean Ethics*. Trans. Irwin, Terence. Indianapolis: Hackett Publishing Company, Inc., 1999.

Berkovits, Eliezer. "An Integrated Jewish World View." *Tradition* (Fall 1962): 5–17.

Berkovits, Eliezer. *Crisis and Faith*. New York: Sanhedrin Press, 1975.

Berkovits, Eliezer. "From the Temple to Synagogue and Back." *Judaism* (Fall 1959): 303–311.

Berkovits, Eliezer. *God, Man and History*. Jerusalem: Shalem Press, 2004.

Berkovits, Eliezer. "Jewish Education in a World Adrift." *Tradition* (Fall 1970): 5–12.

Berkovits, Eliezer. *Jewish Women in Time and Torah*. Hoboken: KTAV Publishing House, Inc., 1990.

Berkovits, Eliezer. *Judaism – Fossil or Ferment?* New York: Philosophical Library. 1956.

Berkovits, Eliezer. *Major Themes in Modern Philosophies of Judaism*. New York: KTAV Publishing House, Inc., 1974.

Berkovits, Eliezer. *Man and God*. Detroit: Wayne State University Press, 1969.

Berkovits, Eliezer. *Not in Heaven*. Hoboken: KTAV Publishing House, Inc., 1983.

Berkovits, Eliezer. "The Galut of Judaism." *Judaism* (January 1953): 225–234.

Berkovits, Eliezer. "The Role of Halakha: Authentic Judaism and Halakha." *Judaism* (Winter 1970): 66–76.

Berkovits, Eliezer. "What is Jewish Philosophy?" *Tradition* (Spring 1961): 117–130.

Berry, George. "Logic with Platonism." *Words and Objections: Essays on the Work of W.V. Quine,* edited by D. Davidson and J. Hintikka. New York: Humanities Press, 1970.

Besdin, Abraham R. *Reflections of the Rav.* Jerusalem: Ahva Co-op Press, 1979.

Breuer, Mordechai. *Pirqe Bereshit.* Alon Shevut: Tevunot Press, 1998.

Byron, George. "Don Juan." *Lord Byron: The Complete Poetical Works,* vol. 5, Edited by Jerome J. McGann. New York: Oxford University Press. 1986.

Calaprice, Alice, ed. *The Expanded Quotable Einstein.* Princeton: Princeton University Press, 2000.

Epstein, Joseph. *Shiurei HaRav.* Hoboken: KTAV Publishing House, 1974.

Feldman, Aharon. *The Juggler and the King.* New York: Feldheim Publishers, 1990.

Fox, Marvin. "The Unity and Structure of Rabbi Joseph B. Soloveitchik's Thought." *Tradition* (Winter 1989): 44–64.

Frege, Gottlob. *The Foundations of Arithmetic.* Trans. J. L. Austin. 2nd ed. Oxford: Basil Blackwell, 1968.

Gödel, Kurt. "What is Cantor's continuum problem?" *Philosophy of Mathematics,* edited by P. Benacerraf and H. Putnman. 2nd ed. Cambridge: Cambridge University Press, 1982.

Ha-Levi, Judah. *The Kuzari.* Trans. Hartwig Hirschfeld. New York: Shocken Books, Inc., 1964.

Hazony, David. "Eliezer Berkovits and the Revival of Jewish Moral Thought." *Azure* (Summer 2001): 23–65.

Hazony, David. "Faith after the Holocaust." *Essential Essays on Judaism.* Jerusalem: Shalem Press, 2002.

Hirsch, Samson Raphael, and Joseph Elias. *The Nineteen Letters.* Jerusalem: Feldheim Publishers, 1995.

Hirsch, Samson Raphael, and Isaac Levy. *The Pentateuch: Deuteronomy.* Gateshead: Judaica Press, 1982.

Hirsch, Samson Raphael. *Collected Writings of Rabbi Samson Raphael Hirsch* Volume VII: Jewish Education. New York: P. Feldheim, 1992.

Ibn Pakuda, Bahya. *Duties of the Heart.* Trans. Daniel Haberman. New York: Feldheim Publishers, 1996.

Ibn Yusuf, Saadia. *The Book of Beliefs and Opinions.* Trans. Samuel Rosenblatt. New Haven: Yale University Press, 1948.

Kant, Immanuel. *Fundamental Principles of the Metaphysics of Morals.* Trans. Thomas K. Abbot. Upper Saddle River: Prentice Hall, Inc., 1949.

Kant, Immanuel. *Religion within the Boundaries of Mere Reason.* Trans. Allen Wood. Cambridge: Cambridge University Press, 1998.

Kaplan, Lawrence. "Rabbi Joseph B. Soloveitchik's Philosophy of Halakha." *The Jewish Law Annual,* vol. 7. Boston: Harwood Academic Publishers, 1988.

Lamm, Norman. *Torah Lishmah: Torah for Torah's Sake in the Works of Rabbi Hayyim of Volozhin and His Contemporaries.* New York: Michael Scharf Publication Trust of the Yeshiva University Press, 1989.

Liebman, Charles S. "Orthodoxy in American Jewish Life." *American Jewish Year Book 1965.* Edited by Morris Fine and Milton Himmelfarb. New York: American Jewish Committee, 1965.

Maimonides, Moses. *The Guide for the Perplexed.* Trans. M. Friedlander. New York: Dover Publications, Inc., 1956.

Maimonides, Moses, and Shlomo Pines. *The Guide of the Perplexed.* 1963. Chicago: University of Chicago Press, 1979.

Margenau, H., and R.A. Varghese, eds. *Cosmos, Bios, Theos: Scientists Reflect on Science, God, and the Origins of the Universe, Life, and Homo Sapiens.* LaSalle: Open Court Publishing Co., 1992.

Nolt, John E. "Mathematical Intuition." *Philosophy and Phenomenology Research* (December 1983): 189–211.

Rawls, John. *A Theory of Justice.* Oxford: Oxford University Press, 2000.

Rousseau, Jean Jacques. *The Social Contract.* Trans. Cranston, Maurice. London: Penguin Books, 1968.

Sheler, J.L., and J.M. Schrof. "The Creation." *U.S. News & World Report.* December 23, 1991: 56–64.

Soloveitchik, Joseph Dov, David Shatz, Joel B. Wolowelsky, and Reuven Ziegler. *Abraham's Journey: Reflections on the Life of the Founding Patriarch.* Jersey City: Published for Toras HoRav Foundation by KTAV Pub. House, 2008.

Soloveitchik, Joseph Dov, and Netaniel Helfgot. *Community, Covenant, and Commitment: Selected Letters and Communications of Rabbi Joseph B. Soloveitchik.* Jersey City: Published for the Toras HoRav Foundation by Ktav Pub. House, 2005.

Soloveitchik, Joseph Dov, Eli D. Clark, Joel B. Wolowelsky, and Reuven Ziegler. *Days of Deliverance: Essays on Purim and Hanukkah.* New York: Published for the Toras HoRav Foundation by KTAV Pub. House, 2007.

Soloveitchik, Joseph Dov, David Shatz, and Joel B. Wolowelsky. *Family Redeemed: Essays on Family Relationships.* Hoboken: Toras HoRav Foundation, 2000.

Soloveitchik, Joseph Dov, Joel B. Wolowelsky, and Reuven Ziegler. *Festival of Freedom: Essays on Pesah and the Haggadah.* Jersey City: Published for the Toras HoRav Foundation by KTAV Pub. House, 2006.

Soloveitchik, Joseph Dov, David Shatz, Joel B. Wolowelsky, and Reuven Ziegler. *Out of the Whirlwind: Essays on Mourning, Suffering and the Human Condition.* Hoboken: Published for Toras HoRav Foundation by KTAV Publishing House, 2003.

Soloveitchik, Joseph Dov, and Michael S. Berger. *The Emergence of Ethical Man.* Jersey City: Ktav Pub. House, 2005.

Soloveitchik, Joseph Dov, and Jacob J. Schacter. *The Lord Is Righteous in All His Ways: Reflections on the Tish'ah Be-Av Kinot.* Jersey City: Published for Toras HoRav Foundation by KTAV Pub. House, 2006.

Soloveitchik, Joseph Dov, and Shalom Carmy. *Worship of the Heart: Essays on Jewish Prayer.* Hoboken: Published for Toras HoRav Foundation by KTAV Pub. House, 2003.

Soloveitchik, Joseph B. *Be-Sod ha-Yahad ve-ha-Yahid.* Ed. Pinchas Peli. Jerusalem: World Zionist Organization, 1976.

Soloveitchik, Joseph B. "Catharsis." *Tradition* (Spring 1978): 38–54.

Soloveitchik, Joseph B. "Confrontation." *Tradition* (Spring–Summer 1964): 5–29.

Soloveitchik, Joseph B. *Fate and Destiny.* Hoboken: KTAV Publishing House, 2000.

Soloveitchik, Joseph B. *Halakhic Man.* Philadelphia: The Jewish Publication Society, 1983.

Soloveitchik, Joseph B. *Lonely Man of Faith.* Northvale: Jason Aronson Inc., 1997.

Soloveitchik, Joseph B. *The Halakhic Mind.* New York: Seth Press, 1986.

Soloveitchik, Joseph B. "*U-Vikashtem mi-Sham.*" *Ha-Darom* (1978): 1–83.

Spero, Shubert. "Rabbi Joseph Dov Soloveitchik and the Role of the Ethical." *Modern Judaism* February 2003: 12–31.

Peli, Pinchas. *On Repentance.* Ramsey: Paulist Press, 1984.

Weiss, Raymond L. and Charles E. Butterworth, eds. *Ethical Writings of Maimonides.* New York: Dover Publications, Inc., 1975.

About the Author

Rabbi Ira Bedzow received rabbinical ordination from Rabbi Zalman Nehemiah Goldberg and Rabbi Daniel Channen. He has a Bachelor of Arts degree from Princeton University and a Master of Arts degree from University of Chicago. Rabbi Bedzow is a member of the faculty at Touro College South and the Director of Land Acquisition and Finance at Groupe Pacific.